WATER: A Resource in Crisis

WATER:

A Resource in Crisis

Eileen Lucas

Educational Consultant
Helen J. Challand, Ph.D.
Professor of Science Education, National-Louis University

Technical Consultant
Jim Gilbert
Education Director, The Freshwater Foundation

ℚ CHILDRENS PRESS®
CHICAGO

A production of B&B Publishing, Inc.

Project Editor: Jean Blashfield Black
Designer: Elizabeth B. Graf
Cover Design: Margrit Fiddle
Artist: Valerie A. Valusek

Computer Makeup: Dori Bechtel
Dave Conant
Photo Researcher: Terri Willis
Research Assistant: Marjorie Benson
Research Consultant: Colleen Shine

Printed on Evergreen Gloss
50% recycled preconsumer waste
Binder's board made from 100% recycled material

Library of Congress Cataloging-in-Publication Data

Lucas, Eileen
    Water: a resource in crisis / Eileen Lucas
        p. cm. -- (Saving planet earth)
    Includes index.
    Summary: Discusses how human activities and carelessness are polluting
Earth's water supply and what must be done to clean it up.
    ISBN 0-516-05509-7
    1. Water--Pollution--Juvenile literature. 2. Water conservation--Juvenile
literature. 3. Water quality--Juvenile literature. 4. Water-supply--Juvenile
literature. [1. Water--Pollution. 2. Water conservation. 3. Pollution.] I. Title.
II. Series.
TD422.L83 1991
363.73'94--dc20

                    91-36137
                    CIP
                    AC

Cover photo—© Imtek Imagineering/Masterfile

TABLE OF CONTENTS

Chapter 1

The Crisis in Quantity and Quality

A FAMILY STANDS IN LINE at a well. They are waiting to have the buckets they hold filled with water. After several hours, their turn comes, and then they trudge home with their heavy load, careful not to spill any of the precious liquid. It is all the water they'll get today, and perhaps all they'll get for a week.

Chances are good that such a situation is taking place somewhere in the world right now. It may be happening in India, Mexico, China, Ethiopia, or even in the United States. There are many, many places around the world where people simply do not have enough water. Perhaps they live in an area that is experiencing drought (a long period with little or no rain), or perhaps they live where water sources are polluted. People who serve in Third World countries for the United States Peace Corps tell of mothers who must decide whether to give their babies polluted water or let them die of thirst.

The water resource is in crisis. There is not enough water at the right time, in the right place, and of sufficient quality to meet the needs of the people. Sometimes the crisis is due to natural conditions such as drought, and sometimes it is due to the mismanagement of water by people. Often both are involved.

Discovering We Had a Problem

Water crises are nothing new, but in the past they were caused mostly by nature. In recent years they have been brought on both by nature and by human activities. As one shocking event followed another, even North Americans discovered that water could harm us.

In many countries around the world, it's the task of the children to fetch water from the nearest well or river. Each drop of the precious load is handled with care.

A Problem of Minerals. Calistoga, California, about 50 miles (81 kilometers) north of San Francisco, is a town that has become famous for its water. People go there to take mineral baths at its health spas, and its pure spring water is bottled and sold all over the United States.

But the very minerals that make this water so appealing to some people make it less than satisfactory to others. Therefore the town must get its public drinking water from sources other than its famous mineral springs. And after four consecutive years of drought, Calistoga's water supply is drying up. Citizens are encouraged to conserve water. New construction, which would increase water demand, has been halted. As truckloads of mineral water leave town in 10-ounce (0.3-liter) bottles, the residents of Calistoga face water rationing as well as higher water bills.

A Burning River. The Cuyahoga River, which empties into Lake Erie near Cleveland, Ohio, provides a dramatic example of why there is a crisis in the quality of our water.

Before the cities along the shores of the Cuyahoga and Lake Erie were founded, this was a beautiful wilderness area. As the number of people and buildings and industries grew, so did the problem of waste.

During the 1800s, human sewage was often dumped untreated into the river. Epidemics of typhoid fever, caused by drinking water contaminated with bacteria, were common and deadly. As early as 1868, Cleveland newspapers reported on the "filthy looking conditions of the river."

The cities of Cleveland and Akron grew rapidly along the banks of the Cuyahoga as industries were attracted by the abundance of water. By 1900 Cleveland had become one

of the leading oil-refining and iron- and steel-making centers of the world. In Akron the rubber industry was growing. These industries and many others used the Cuyahoga River as a dumping ground for their wastes.

By the 1950s, the Cuyahoga River was being treated as little more than an open sewer, and that's the way it looked and smelled. Organic matter decaying in the river produced gas that bubbled to the surface like witches' brew. In 1954 the river was tested to measure the amount of dissolved oxygen in the water. Without at least 4 milligrams of oxygen per liter of water, plant and animal life cannot survive. But for 20 of the 43 miles (32 of the 69 kilometers) between Akron and Cleveland the Cuyahoga contained no dissolved oxygen at all. The bacteria count in some places was higher than that of untreated sewage. In 1952 the Cuyahoga River caught fire and burned for several days. Fires continued to break out over the years including 1959, when floating oil and solid material caused it to burn for eight days. In 1969, fires were still occurring on the Cuyahoga.

The citizens of Cleveland and Akron took to the streets, demanding that the river be cleaned up. As the 1960s progressed, people all over the world became more aware of the disgraceful condition of many lakes and rivers. The Cuyahoga was just one flaming example of what was happening.

A lot of things happened between 1952 (left) and 1988 (right) on the Cuyahoga River in Ohio. The river that was so polluted it caught on fire was cleaned up, making the river a pleasant place for boating.

Strange Things in the Water. The Grand Calumet River, which runs into the southern tip of Lake Michigan via the Indiana Canal, was so loaded with steel-mill wastes including grease and oil that it looked and flowed like melted chocolate. For years, studies showed that the river contained no oxygen and was virtually lifeless.

In Green Bay, Wisconsin, all the city beaches had been closed due to pollution since 1943. The pollution came from paper mills located upstream on the Fox River. These mills used the river to dump their wastes, which were loaded with toxic (poisonous) chemicals such as chlorine and mercury. The Fox River had once been known for its great catches of walleye pike, but by the 1950s it could boast of very few edible fish.

In 1965 New York City found itself almost without any drinkable water. There was plenty of water in the area—the Hudson River flows through a large section of the city. But sewage and industrial pollution had made it undrinkable. The only fish that lived in the river was an eel that survived on human waste.

We Harmed Our Own Water

Most of these problems were caused by the dumping of sewage and industrial waste into surface waters (lakes, streams, and rivers). These wastes kill fish and make water unsafe to drink. And drinking contaminated water can cause such

A milky "river" of industrial wastes containing chlorine, dioxin, PCBs, and heavy metals from the paper industry flows into the Fox River in Wisconsin.

human ailments as skin rashes, head-
aches, stomach aches, and sore throats.
Long-term effects are difficult to
prove, but evidence links continued
drinking of contaminated water with
liver and kidney disorders, deaths of
unborn babies (miscarriages), birth
defects, cancer, and death.

Even as our waterways were becoming clogged with
pollution, we were discovering that water pumped from the
ground could be contaminated, too. In a neighborhood
called Love Canal, near Niagara Falls, New York, people
were getting sick. As early as 1958 there were reports of
children suffering burns after playing in the school play-
ground. Investigators found an unusually high number of
birth defects and leukemia and other cancers among the
residents. Eventually it was discovered that 21,500 tons
(19,350 metric tons) of chemical waste had been buried on
the site in 1947. The drums (barrels) of chemicals had been
covered with clay and dirt, and homes were built above
them. Then the drums began to leak. Fumes escaped into the
air, and the chemicals seeped into the water that filled local
wells. The people of Love Canal had been unknowingly
drinking this contaminated water.

As if that weren't bad enough, we then discovered that
even rainwater could be polluted. Industrial smokestacks
belched poisons into the sky in cities across the nation. Rain
and snowfall picked up these poisons and deposited them
in lakes and rivers, forests and farmlands. Virtually every
aspect of Earth's great water resource was being contaminated. Something had to be done.

Some factories have made a habit of discharging hazardous wastes directly into a river or lake. Now we know that the usefulness of water can be destroyed that way.

Well, something has been done. Approximately $1 billion has been spent cleaning up wastewater dumped into the Cuyahoga River alone. Industries and sewage-treatment plants have been given standards that their wastewater must meet. They try to conserve water and recycle used water as much as possible. In all but the last several miles of the Cuyahoga River the dissolved oxygen level is now well above the minimum for health. Levels of many contaminants have gone down. Today, the river looks and smells much better and people are once again able to enjoy boating and recreation along the Cuyahoga.

The same is true for many of the rivers so badly polluted in the 1960s. The Fox River looks and smells noticeably better. An occasional walleye can be found swimming in its waters once again. The Grand Calumet River is cleaned up enough that some carp and shiners venture into it. As a water-quality engineer remarked, "It's not a healthy population, but it's certainly an improvement."

An improvement, yes. But these rivers are not yet clean. Decades of abuse cannot be washed away that easily. Even if these rivers look better, millions of tons of dissolved poisons remain in sediment in the river bottoms.

And there are still people and companies that treat rivers and lakes like toilets. In 1988 a sewage-treatment plant on the Mississippi River was sued by the United States government for discharging raw sewage into the river. And in late 1989 an oil-refining company was charged with dumping ammonia, oil, grease, and other pollutants into the Mississippi. The company is now being forced to spend $50 million to improve the way it handles wastewater.

And the pollution of groundwater is even more difficult—and extremely expensive—to clean up. In some cases, it is virtually impossible to clean underground water once it is contaminated. Wells must simply be closed down. Almost every state in the country has had some wells closed because of groundwater contamination.

Adopting a Waterway

An Earth Experience

Is there a stream, creek, pond, river, or lake in your area? Spend some time studying it.

Is there much water movement? This is a factor in determining oxygen content, which in turn determines what life forms will be able to survive there. What life forms do you see—on the shores and in the water? Observe any relationships between plants and animals. Are there life forms present that you cannot see? Take some water samples and study them under a microscope.

What is the bottom like—sand, mud, stone, etc.? How clear is the water? How deep is it? What is the temperature? What is the pH? Use acid-measuring paper (ask your science teacher where you can get some) to find out. A pH between 6 and 8 is best for a variety of life forms.

Is the water sheltered by trees or bushes? Does it get much sunlight? Are there changes over time? Is this ecosystem polluted? What can you do to help it?

Our modern society is incredibly thirsty. We want more water all the time. The vast amounts of water that we thought were ours for all time are becoming scarce or polluted. What we put in the air and on the ground affects our water supplies. And this life-giving resource is in crisis.

Chapter 2

Earth's Water Resources

THE PLANET EARTH IS CALLED "the Blue Planet" because two-thirds of it is covered with water. So can there possibly be a water crisis?

Yes, there can. And there are two major reasons for this. The first has to do with quality.

Much of the water that covers the Earth is the salt water of the oceans, which humans cannot drink. It makes us sick and damages the tissues in our bodies. Much of the Earth's fresh water, the water found in lakes and rivers, is polluted with bacteria and chemicals that make it hazardous to the health of people who drink it. A shortage of water can occur when water supplies are unfit for human use.

The second reason has to do with location—having enough water where it is needed. It is very expensive to move large amounts of water great distances, so while some places have plenty of water, other places may have water shortages.

The study of the distribution and movement of Earth's water resources is called hydrology. A person who studies these aspects of water is a hydrologist.

The Water Cycle

Did you know that there is just about as much water on the planet Earth now as there was during the ancient civilizations of Egypt and China? That's because of the *water cycle*, the Earth's own recycling system. The water cycle is the process by which water moves from the air to the land and back again. It is also known as the *hydrologic cycle*. The sun provides the energy that keeps this process in motion.

Precipitation (rain and snow) occurs when water vapor condenses into clouds and falls from the sky. Most of it falls

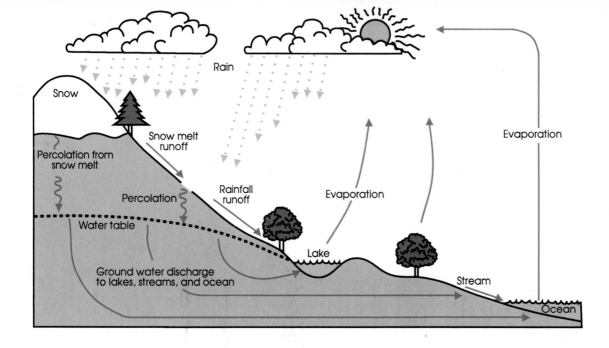

into oceans, lakes, and rivers. The sun's heat evaporates the water back into the atmosphere as water vapor, and it falls to Earth again as precipitation.

Some of the rain and snow that falls on land runs off into rivers, lakes, and other surface waters, replenishing them. Some rain is absorbed from the ground by trees and other plants, which in turn give back some of that moisture to the air in a process called transpiration.

Some water sinks down into the soil, finding its way into the mass of water, called an aquifer, that is stored in porous rock. The top of an aquifer is called the water table. Some of this underground water is pumped to the surface in wells, and some flows into surface water where the water table and lakes and rivers meet. The illustration on pages 18 and 19 shows water in the environment.

So the water supplies of the planet are constantly being recycled and redistributed by means of the water cycle. It is a process that's been going on for millions of years and should continue for millions more.

Except that human beings are messing it up. We interfere with the process several ways. One way is by withdrawing water from a source faster than the water cycle can replenish it. Another is by returning contaminated water to a source, thus polluting that source and perhaps others as well. We will learn more about these problems in later chapters.

The Water Cycle in Action

An Earth Experience

If you've ever seen plants growing in a sealed terrarium, you have seen the water cycle in action. In a terrarium, plants take in moisture from the soil. They also release moisture from their leaves in a process called transpiration. The moisture is given off in the form of water vapor. The vapor condenses, or becomes liquid, on the sides of the terrarium. Then it runs into the soil to be used again.

To set up a terrarium, you will need a glass aquarium with a tight-fitting cover. Place a layer of gravel on the bottom. Cover this with a layer of peat moss and then a layer of dirt. Plant some small plants in the dirt. Ferns and mosses work well.

Lightly water the plants so that the soil is moist but not completely soaked. Cover the terrarium. If the terrarium has been properly constructed, you should not have to add more water. The water cycle within the aquarium will recycle the water in this mini-ecosystem over and over again.

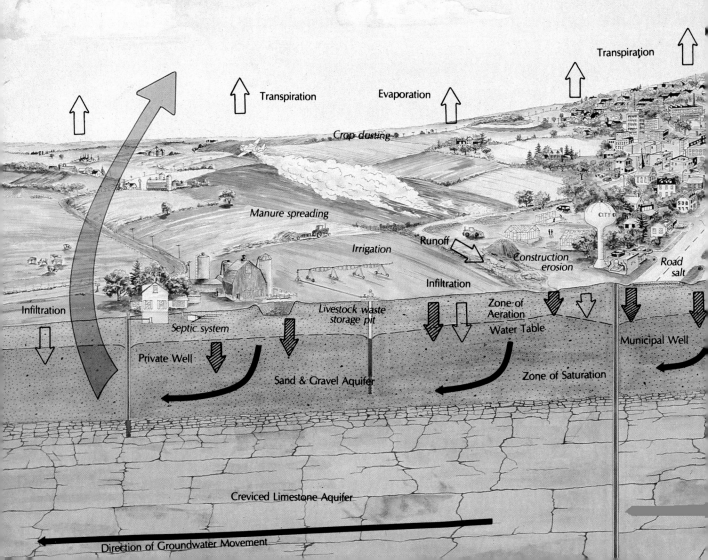

Direction of Groundwater Movement

Human induced impacts on groundwater

Natural processes

Transpiration

Transpiration

Evaporation

Crop dusting

Manure spreading

Runoff

Irrigation

Construction erosion

Infiltration

Road salt

Infiltration

Zone of Aeration

Livestock waste storage pit

Septic system

Water Table

Private Well

Municipal Well

Sand & Gravel Aquifer

Zone of Saturation

Creviced Limestone Aquifer

Direction of Groundwater Movement

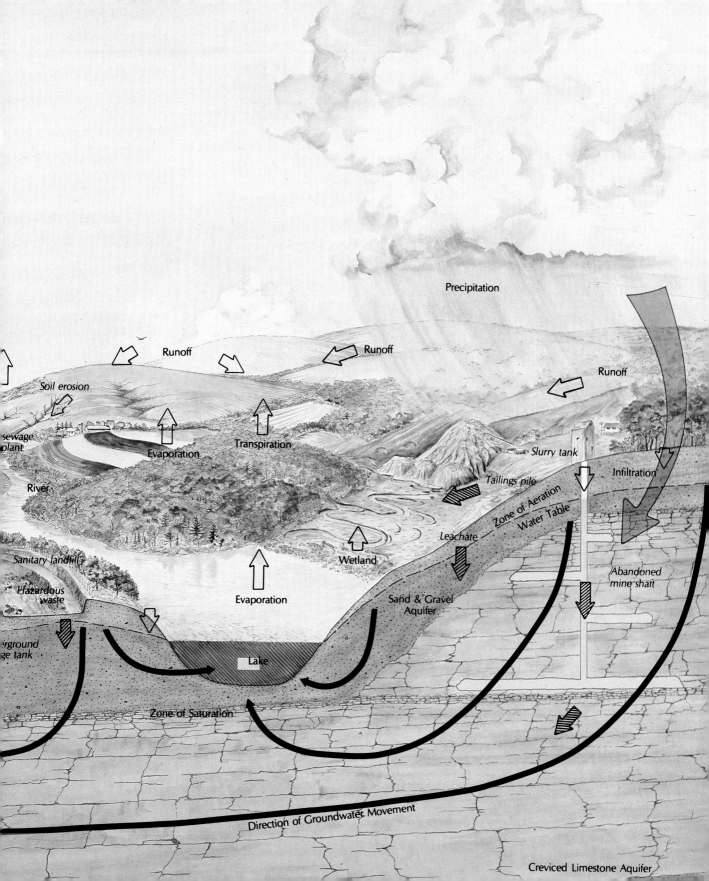

Precipitation

Runoff

Runoff

Runoff

Soil erosion

sewage
plant

Evaporation

Transpiration

Slurry tank

Infiltration

Tailings pile

River

Leachate

Zone of Aeration

Water Table

Sanitary landfill

Wetland

Abandoned
mine shaft

Hazardous
waste

Evaporation

Sand & Gravel
Aquifer

rground
ge tank

Lake

Zone of Saturation

Direction of Groundwater Movement

Creviced Limestone Aquifer

In northern countries, winter snow melts in the spring, replenishing, or refilling, the water source.

Water in the Air

Water is present in the atmosphere in three forms: precipitation, water vapor, and clouds. Precipitation occurs when water comes down as rain or snow—in a liquid or frozen state. Water vapor is the water molecule (H_2O) in a gaseous state. It results from evaporation and transpiration.

Precipitation is obviously a key part of the water cycle. Where rainfall is abundant, plants grow and the Earth is green. Rivers flow and lakes form. Where precipitation is slight, there are fewer plants and less surface water.

The amount of rainfall varies dramatically in different parts of the world. It ranges from over 400 inches (1,000 centimeters) per year in northeastern India to only about 10 inches (25 centimeters) per year in desert regions.

The overall average rainfall in the United States is 30 inches (75 centimeters) of precipitation annually. But that figure tells you little about how much rain any given area will receive. For example, in parts of the Pacific Northwest of the United States, rainfall averages between 150 and 200 inches (375 and 500 centimeters) per year. Parts of the Pacific Southwest receive less than 5 inches (12.5 centimeters). Death Valley, California, generally records only about 1 1/2 inches (3.75 centimeters) of rain each year.

Three-fourths of all the precipitation that falls in North
America is evaporated or transpired back into the atmosphere. The rest runs off into oceans, lakes, and rivers or
seeps down into the soil.

Water in vapor form is also of great importance to human life. Without moisture in the air, we would not be able
to breathe. Our lungs must be kept continually moist in
order to work. Water vapor is also an important part of the
water cycle. Without water evaporating there would be none
to fall. Most evaporation takes place over the oceans, but a
great deal of water evaporates from freshwater surfaces like
lakes and streams and reservoirs, as well as from the land
itself after rain falls.

*A greatly enlarged view
of a raindrop hitting a
solid surface.*

21

Each day, 1 acre (0.4 hectare) of corn sends over 3,000 gallons (11,400 liters) of water into the atmosphere through transpiration. During the course of a year, a large oak tree will transpire about 40,000 gallons (152,000 liters) of water.

Some water vapor rises in the air and collects in clouds, where it condenses back into liquid or frozen form, and the cycle goes on and on. The fact that sun-warmed air is trapped below clouds helps to keep the Earth warm. When temperature, wind, and other conditions are right, the vapor in the air condenses, or becomes a liquid, and is pulled to the ground by gravity as rain or snow.

These layered altocumulus clouds show one of the many varieties of clouds that water vapor in the sky can form, depending on temperature, winds, and air pressure.

As you sip a cold drink from a glass on a hot day, you may notice drops of water forming on the outside of the glass. It seems almost as if water is coming through the glass, but that water comes from the air. Hot air holds more water than cold air, so as the air right next to your icy drink cools, some of the water vapor in it condenses, becoming liquid drops of water on the glass. This is the principle that operates in precipitation.

There is constantly water in the air, either rising into the air in vapor form through transpiration and evaporation, or coming down through precipitation. The sun, the wind, the shape of the land, and many other factors combine to keep moisture in the air.

22

97%

Water on the Ground

Although the Earth can claim billions of gallons of water at all three levels (air, surface, and underground), less than 1 percent is usable fresh water. The rest is mostly salt water or water that is bound up in glacial ice and snow. But even though fresh water makes up only a small percentage of the Earth's total volume of water, there is still a huge quantity of it.

The world's water supply exists in oceans (right), *lakes* (below—in Chicago), *and glaciers* (below right—in Alaska). *Less than 1 percent is fresh water, and 97 percent of that is underground.*

2.15%

.65%

Oceans   Glaciers   Freshwater

Surface fresh water, found in lakes, rivers, and streams, makes up only a very small portion of the planet's total supply of water. But it has played a very important role in history.

People have always depended on fresh water. Throughout history civilizations have grown up and flourished along the shores of freshwater sources—the Sumerians in Mesopotamia, the Egyptians along the Nile. In the United States and Canada, too, cities were often founded on the shores of lakes and rivers. These waterways served to connect cities with one another, and the water itself was needed for many purposes. Paris on the Seine River and Chicago on Lake Michigan are two examples of cities strategically located on fresh water.

Rivers. The land from which water drains into a particular river is called that river's watershed. One watershed is separated from another by land that is higher than its surroundings. This higher land, called a divide, makes surface water flow in a particular direction. Regional watersheds are grouped in larger categories, called continental watersheds, which are separated by continental divides.

FACT

There are some 3.25 million miles (5.2 million kilometers) of rivers in the United States alone. The Mississippi River— North America's longest river—is 2,348 miles (3,780 kilometers) long. The Mackenzie—the longest river in Canada—is 1,060 miles (1,707 kilometers) long. The Amazon, in South America, is almost 4,000 miles (6,440 kilometers) long.

The mouth of the Klamath River in California. The river has been declared "wild and scenic," which protects it from development.

Sometimes people have decided to change the natural flow of rivers. This may be done for many reasons. In Canada, it is often done so that water can be stored behind dams to produce electric power. In the American West, it is often done for irrigation. In Chicago, the course of the Chicago River was changed for navigation and sewage-disposal reasons. In many places, rivers are diverted to bring water where people want it. Then people elsewhere on the river may lose water, and this can lead to serious problems.

The volume of water in a river and the speed with which it flows affect how the river is used. We use rivers as major highways (like the Mississippi), as power generators (like the Columbia), as sewer systems (like the Chicago), and as water-delivery systems (like the Colorado).

The speed with which water flows in a river is affected by both the amount of water in the river and the slope of the land. A fast-moving river has more effect on the land around it than a slow-moving one. Over thousands of years, a river can sculpt out wide valleys and deep canyons. The flow of water—one of the greatest sculptors of all times—has cre-

The Mississippi is a working river that provides transportation to the heart of the United States. Thousands of barges carrying goods travel its waters every day.

ated dramatic landscapes both above and below the surface of the Earth.

Lakes. A lake is a large inland body of water. It can be part of a river system. That is, a lake is often a place where a river widens. One of the main functions of a lake is to act as a reservoir. Lakes store water during times of abundant rainfall and release it gradually into a river or rivers.

FACT

Canada has 565 lakes larger than 38 square miles (about 100 square kilometers), probably more lake area than any other country in the world. The Great Lakes, which form part of the border between the United States and Canada, contain about 18 percent of the world's fresh surface water.

One of the biggest problems that occurs in lakes is increased salinity (salt content) caused by evaporation across their large surfaces. As water evaporates, salt and other minerals are left behind. In some lakes, the process is very, very slow and gradual, a normal process that happens over centuries. In others, it has been speeded up by human activities. The Aral Sea, for example, is a huge inland lake in the

Soviet Union. It is shrinking rapidly because large quantities of water are being removed for irrigation (watering crops). The water that remains is contaminated with salts and pesticides. The people living nearby suffer from stomach problems, typhoid, and throat cancer, all of which have been linked to drinking contaminated water.

Another problem for many lakes is that they slowly fill by sediment—soil washed from the land with rainfall. In areas where poor land-use practices increase the amount of soil flowing into a lake, the lake slowly fills up with sediment. Because that sediment can block the lake's inlet and outlet, the lake may eventually become a pond or marsh.

Streams, Creeks, and Wetlands. Streams and creeks are small bodies of flowing water. Wetlands include marshes, wet meadows, bogs, small ponds, swamps, and fens. They are basically land areas where the water table is very close to—if not level with—the surface of the land.

About half of America's wetlands have been destroyed by draining and filling since the founding of the United States. And the destruction of wetlands has taken place in many other places around the world.

Many people have become aware of the important role that wetlands have in the environment and are now trying to halt this trend. Among the many benefits of wetlands is their ability to purify polluted waters. They also act as reservoirs for storm

Lake Superior is one of the largest bodies of fresh water in the world.

A bog is a wetland area with spongy soil that has become waterlogged. Certain mosses and other plants like those conditions.

water, which eases flooding. And they provide homes and breeding grounds for birds and other wildlife, many of which have become endangered as the world's wetlands disappear.

Water Under the Ground

If you dig deep enough, almost any hole will produce water. In the moist areas of the northeastern United States, you will probably have to dig no more than 20 feet (6 meters) to find water. Around Tucson, Arizona, you may have to dig at least ten times that far, but even in that hot, dry region, there is water available underground.

About 97 percent of the Earth's supply of fresh water is underground. This vast water resource is known as groundwater. In some countries of the world, such as Israel and Saudi Arabia, almost all of the population's freshwater needs are met by groundwater. Wells and the water they supply are growing in number and importance around the globe—from India and North Africa to the American West.

Groundwater is an extremely valuable natural resource. About two-thirds of the groundwater pumped to the surface in the United States is used for irrigation. The rest is divided

A pumping station in California (left) lifts water from sea level to 3,300 feet (990 meters) above sea level to an aqueduct that carries water to a huge agricultural area. In Senegal, Africa (right), the raising of the water is done by human power.

between industrial and residential use. While some states are more dependent than others on groundwater, every state relies on this resource to some extent. Fifty percent of the American people get their drinking water from groundwater sources. In Hawaii, 90 percent of drinking water is groundwater. Several American cities, including Long Island, New York, rely on groundwater for all their drinking-water needs. Even in Canada, where there is such an abundance of surface water, 25 percent of the people rely on groundwater for home water supplies. On Prince Edward Island, off the coast of Nova Scotia, all household water needs are supplied by groundwater.

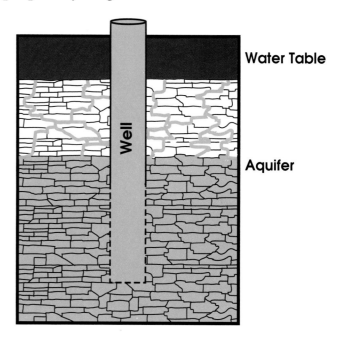

Groundwater is part of the water cycle. It starts out as precipitation that falls to the Earth and seeps through the particles of soil that make up the outer layer of the planet. Some of the groundwater that we use today fell as rain hundreds and even thousands of years ago.

Rain filters down through various layers of soil until it reaches a water-saturated zone. In the upper layers of soil, some spaces are filled with water, some with air. In the water-saturated zone, all spaces between soil grains are filled with water. The top of this water-saturated zone is called the water table. The part of the zone below the water table is known as an aquifer.

The Water Table

To demonstrate the water table, you will need a large, wide-mouthed glass jar. Fill the jar at least two-thirds full with a mixture of sand and gravel. Slowly pour water in the jar until about half the sand/gravel mix is saturated. Mark the side of the jar where the saturated zone ends. This is the water table.

Add a little more water to simulate heavy rainfall. What happens to the water table? If you leave your jar uncovered for an extended period of time (several weeks) to simulate drought, what happens to the water table? (Some of the water evaporates, and the water table drops.)

Aquifers. Aquifers are geologic formations that store and transmit water. That is, they are underground areas that hold water like reservoirs, and they allow this water to move from place to place.

Two factors that determine whether rock is a good aquifer are porosity and permeability. *Porosity* is the amount of space between grains or pores of the rock. Sand and gravel are very porous — they have many openings and much space between grains. *Permeability* is the ability of water to move through the rock. The pores, or openings, between grains must be connected for the rock to be permeable. Limestone, a rock that is not very porous, can be permeable when cracks connect the openings and allow water to run through. And while clay can sometimes be very porous, it is not considered permeable because the openings are so small that water movement is very slow.

People used to think that water flowed underground in swift, clear rivers. Now we know that while groundwater does move, it usually does not travel very far or very quickly. Like surface water, it generally flows downward, following the most permeable path through layers of sand, gravel, and rock. It can move anywhere from 1 inch to about 3 feet (2.5 centimeters to 0.9 meters) per day.

There are basically two ways for water in an aquifer to reach the surface. In natural discharge, groundwater flows into a lake or spring and thus becomes surface water. In human-induced discharge, wells are dug to bring groundwater to the surface where it can be used.

Aquifers can be either unconfined or confined. In an unconfined aquifer, water filters down through the soil until it reaches the level of saturation—the water table. Impermeable materials below the aquifer stop the water in the aquifer from seeping down any lower. Somewhere below this layer

When new houses or other buildings are built beyond city limits, a well usually has to be dug to provide water to the structure. The drilling apparatus goes deep into the aquifer below the building.

of impermeable material, called an aquitard, may be another level of rock saturated with water. That second region of water is called a confined aquifer because it is bounded by an impermeable aquitard both above and below. If the pressure in this confined aquifer is great enough, a well drilled into it will have water that flows upward without any mechanical assistance (pumping). Such a well is called an artesian well.

Where soil is porous and permeable, and rainfall is frequent and heavy, precipitation easily works its way through the soil to an aquifer. The water table is likely to be fairly close to the surface and the aquifer below it is easily recharged.

About half of all the water that is underground is within $1/2$ mile (0.8 kilometer) of the Earth's surface. Therefore, it can be reached fairly easily by modern drilling methods. But the top of any aquifer—the water table—can change from season to season or year to year and may drop drastically with large withdrawals.

One of the basic laws of water use is that the amount of water withdrawn from a source must not exceed the amount deposited. In this way, the water table remains stable. Unfortunately, this law is often broken.

FACT

Since 1950, groundwater use in the United States has risen from 34 billion gallons (129 billion liters) every day to 89 billion gallons (338 billion liters) every day in 1980. Two-thirds of this water is used in irrigation. The rest is divided between public and industrial use.

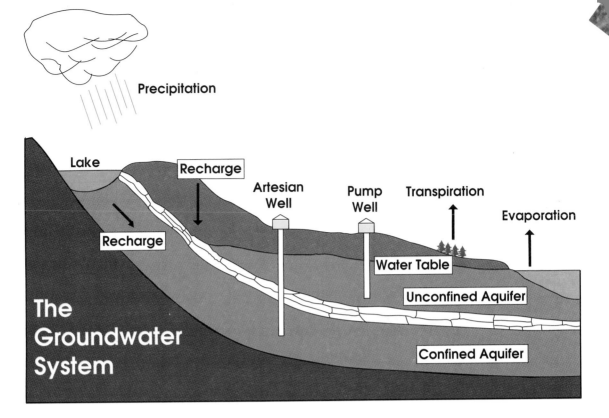

Precipitation

The Groundwater System

Lake

Recharge

Recharge

Artesian Well

Pump Well

Transpiration

Evaporation

Water Table

Unconfined Aquifer

Confined Aquifer

As the use of groundwater has increased, so has the abuse. Groundwater is being contaminated more and more often. We will see how many aquifers are being destroyed by pollution and overuse. Growing numbers of individuals and groups are getting involved in the protection of this vital resource. Ultimately, it is up to all of us to protect our water resources, in the air, on the surface, and underground.

Folsom Lake near Sacramento was at only 50 percent of its capacity in 1991 because of serious drought conditions in California.

33

Chapter 3

The Many Ways
We Use Water

EVER-INCREASING DEMANDS upon the world's freshwater sources are constantly being made. Modern society seems to find new uses for this precious resource all the time, and worldwide population increases mean these demands are being made by more and more people.

Of all the water used in the United States, about 47 percent is used in agriculture, 44 percent in industry, and only 9 percent in households. Of that 9 percent, only a small portion is actually used for drinking. In Canada, only about 8 percent of water withdrawals are used for irrigation. The largest users of Canadian water are energy production and manufacturing facilities.

Americans use more water per person than citizens of any other country in the world. According to the United States Geological Survey, about 450 billion gallons (1,710 billion liters) of water are used in this country each day. That amounts to approximately 2,000 gallons (7,600 liters) per person per day. This is more than double the amount of water that was being used in 1950. By contrast, in some of the very poor, undeveloped countries of the world, water use per person is as low as 10 gallons (38 liters) per day.

Now you're probably thinking that you don't use anywhere near that much water. And you're right. You don't. This figure includes water being used on farms, in factories, and in other places of business all over the country. It is used to grow the food you eat; to cool your house, school, and supermarket; to generate the energy that runs the lights and appliances in your home; and to produce virtually all manufactured goods.

And you probably use more water on a daily basis than

An important use of uncontaminated water is recreation. Swimming in polluted water can cause skin problems as well as disease.

you think. Reports show that the average American uses between 50 and 150 gallons (190 and 570 liters) of water at home each day. The higher figure is usually found in warm, dry places where more water is used in the garden and in the operation of air conditioners. By the year 2000, usage in the United States is expected to be over 200 gallons (760 liters) per person per day.

Why Humans Need Water

The human body is made up of about 60 to 70 percent water. (People with a higher percentage of body fat have a lower percentage of water.) Believe it or not, you could probably live for several weeks without any food, but you would last only a few days without water. With a loss of only 5 to 10 percent of the body's water, a person will begin to suffer from dehydration. A loss of 15 percent would most likely be fatal.

Much of the water in the human body is recirculated and used over and over again. However, some fresh water has to be brought in (by eating and drinking) and some water has to be removed (by urination, breathing, and perspiration) each day. The amount we take in and give out must be carefully balanced—neither too much nor too little in or out.

Your body uses water to digest food, maintain body temperature, remove wastes and toxins, cleanse the eyes, lubricate joints, and more. The kidneys use water to purge the body of wastes in the bloodstream. About 2 to 2 1/2 quarts (1.9 to 2.4 liters) of this water and waste is removed from the body as urine each day.

You probably drink a couple of glasses of water each day—more if you live where the climate is dry or hot and if you exert physical energy. Obviously, the water you drink should be clean and free of harmful bacteria or chemicals.

But is it? We'll find out in Chapter 4.

You also take in water from the food you eat. Many foods are composed largely of water.

Beverages such as milk and fruit juice are about 85 to 90 percent water. Other foods high in water content include tomatoes (94 percent), watermelon (93 percent), yogurt (89 percent), and apples (84 percent). Even "dry" foods, like meat, are 50 to 70 percent water, and bread—which seems dry—is about 35 percent water.

But the water you drink and the water in your food is only a very small portion of the water you use.

When you drink milk you are drinking a lot of water, because milk is about 90 percent water. Cows must drink a lot of good-quality water in order to produce good milk.

Household Water

Think of all the ways water is used in your house. If you are a typical American, your water use roughly matches the following table.

Place of Use	Amount of Water Used
Standard toilet	3 to 7 gallons (11 to 27 liters) per flush; average 5 gallons (19 liters) per flush
Water-saving toilet	1.6 gallons (5.7 liters) per flush
Bathtub	30 to 40 gallons (113 to 152 liters)
Shower	20 to 40 gallons (76 to 152 liters)—(6 to 10 gallons (23 to 38 liters) per minute)
Washing machine	20 to 30 gallons (76 to 113 liters) per load of clothes
Kitchen sink	Washing dishes by hand, preparing food — 10 to 20 gallons (38 to 76 liters)
Bathroom sink	Washing hands, shaving, brushing teeth —10 to 20 gallons (38 to 76 liters)

FACT

A dripping faucet that leaks just one drop of water every second will waste 4 gallons (15 liters) of water in a day, which is 1,400 gallons (5,320 liters) over a year. And it would cost only a few dollars to repair.

Then there's the water you use outdoors. This includes watering lawns, flower beds, and vegetable gardens, as well as washing cars and filling swimming pools. Outdoor use varies dramatically from region to region in North America. In Wisconsin, an average of 2 gallons (7.6 liters) per day is used outside the house. This figure is low because heavy use occurs only during the three summer months. In hot, dry places like California and Arizona, some households use over 100 gallons (380 liters) per day outside—all year round.

Keeping a lawn watered may use up more than 36,500 gallons (138,700 liters) of water during the year in a warm, dry climate.

The Nuts and Bolts. Drinking water is extremely cheap in the United States. According to *Consumer Reports*, Americans generally pay between 50 cents and $2 for 1,000 gallons (3,800 liters) of clean drinking water.

But the price you pay for water seldom reflects the true cost of delivering that water to your home and cleaning it up after you use it.

The cost of the water you use includes the cost of digging wells and pumping water, laying water pipes and sewage pipes, and building water-treatment plants. When we turn on a faucet, these billion-dollar industries function behind the scenes.

In most cities, public water systems deliver water to all households. Some public water systems are owned by private investors, but most are owned and operated by local governments. In some systems, each home has a meter and consumers pay for the actual amount of water they use. In other cities, there are no meters, and each household pays a

Part of what people pay for water goes to cleaning up the wastewater after use in order to return it to a water source. This facility is treating the wastewater to remove contaminants.

flat rate. In general, people who pay a flat rate use about twice as much water as those who have their water metered.

Some people get their water from their own well, in which case they don't pay for water at all. They pay only the cost of pumping it into their home.

Federal and state regulations set standards for public water systems. People who have private wells must monitor their own water supply.

Where does your water come from, and how is it paid for?

An Earth Experience

Examining Water Use

The following activities may help you and your family become more aware of water use.

1. Do a water audit in your home. Each morning for a week, check your water meter to see how much water was used in your home the previous day. If you don't have a water meter, you'll have to be more creative about figuring this out. For example, place a large bucket under the shower. Run the water for thirty seconds. Measure the amount of water collected and multiply by two. This tells you how much water your shower uses every minute. Time the showers taken in your home to see how much water is used in just this one way.

2. Learn how water has played a part in the development of your community. Are you located near surface water? When were the first wells dug? Are there heavy water-users nearby such as major businesses or industries?

3. Put together a report or bulletin board about water use. Include articles and pictures from magazines and newspapers. Consider making a display to put in a public place such as the library, city hall, or a shopping center.

Water Used by Towns and Small Businesses

We've looked at water used in homes on a daily basis. But we've only begun to consider the many ways we use it.

Every municipality, whether it's a small village or a large city, uses water. Cities use water for fighting fires, cleaning streets, watering public areas (grass, trees, shrubs, flowers), filling public pools, and supplying public fountains—including drinking fountains in public buildings such as schools and libraries.

The many different businesses within your community also use water. Consider how much water is used by restaurants, hospitals, laundromats and dry cleaners, golf courses, hotels, car washes, beauty and barber shops, gas stations, and health clubs.

Water on Farms

When we think of water on farms, we think first of watering crops, but even the production of meat requires huge amounts of water. Chickens, pigs, and sheep, all the animals

Chickens are only one kind of livestock that requires huge quantities of water to become food on our tables.

of the typical barnyard, need water to stay alive. And their food must be grown. Water is also used in the production of meat for food and in the cooling systems used to keep that meat fresh.

Vegetable and grain crops need water to grow. Water is also used in the application of fertilizers, herbicides, and pesticides that increase crop yield.

Agriculture accounts for much of the water used in the United States and many other countries. And most of the water is used for irrigation, the process of supplying water to crops to compensate for lack of rainfall. Today, about half of all the world's crops rely on irrigation.

The process of irrigation has played a role in the rise and fall of civilizations as far back as the days of Mesopotamia and the pharaohs of Egypt. Some 5,000 years ago, people began building channels to carry water to dry fields. Crude methods of lifting water from low-lying rivers to fields at higher elevations were devised. Over the years, many devices have been created to make water work harder and to make life easier for people.

In 1000 B.C., a farmer with a bucket and a pole could irrigate $1/4$ acre (0.1 hectare) in one day. By A.D. 1000, a farmer using a buffalo to turn a wheel, could irrigate 5 acres (2 hectares) in one day. In some parts of the world, this is still the average.

Irrigation methods used in ancient times (above) may still be used somewhere in the world. In China, rice fields may be watered by a pedal-powered system (above right). In Saudi Arabia, however, the mechanical system has progressed to a huge collection of power-driven sprinklers that move in circles (right), bringing water to what used to be desert waste land.

In the industrialized countries of the world, however, this capability has been far exceeded. Advances in technology such as electric pumps and modern irrigation systems allow farmers to irrigate huge tracts of land. Using such techniques, a farmer can pump up to 1,000 gallons (3,800 liters) of water per minute over a 160-acre (64-hectare) area.

Modern irrigation practices have allowed many thousands of acres of marginal land to become highly productive farmland. Land that could barely supply enough grass to feed a few cows can now grow bushels of food. Thanks in large part to irrigation, over one-third of the agricultural output of the United States is produced for export. And the food that stays at home is plentiful and relatively cheap.

But there is a cost for all this bounty. The miracle of irrigation is made possible by federal subsidies (government

An aqueduct (a man-made river) through farmland carries water to huge areas of the countryside.

How Much Water It Takes

120 gallons (456 liters) to produce one egg

About 26 gallons (99 liters) to produce each ear of corn

About 3,500 gallons (13,300 liters) to produce one pound (0.4 kilogram) of beef

300 gallons (1,140 liters) to produce one loaf of bread

And . . . 1,400 gallons (5,200 liters) are used during the final production of a single fast-food meal of burger, fries, and soft drink

About 12,000 gallons (45,600 liters) to grow a bushel of wheat

payments) that make water cheap for farmers. So expensive water projects are paid for by U.S. taxpayers. Continual tilling of land and planting the same crops year after year cause increased soil erosion and loss of soil nutrients. Alarming quantities of fertilizer and pesticides run off farm fields into surface water and groundwater. An important side effect of modern farming practices is the draining of wetlands and the loss of the animal habitats that go with them. Nonrenewable fossil fuel, such as coal, is used up to provide energy for irrigation systems. The use of fossil fuels results in environmental problems such as acid rain and global warming.

After rain falls on farmland, it may run off into water sources or seep into the ground carrying pesticides, manure, and other fertilizers with it into the groundwater.

Cows and Pesticides. Water is also used to spray crops with fertilizers and pesticides. The water evaporates or soaks into the ground, often carrying the chemical with it.

Livestock need drinking water just as humans do. A cow requires 3 gallons (11.4 liters) of water for each gallon (3.8 liters) of milk it produces. The 1.8 million dairy cows in the state of Wisconsin each drink 45 gallons (171 liters) of water every day. That's 30.2 billion gallons (115 billion liters) a year! Add to this the water used to maintain sanitary conditions in the milk house, not to mention the water used to grow the cows' feed, and you can see that dairy production

needs lots of pure water.

There are a number of things that can be done to reduce the volume of water used in American agriculture and cut down on the damage to the environment, without greatly reducing the production of food. We will learn more about this in Chapter 6.

Power from Water

Power plants are the largest users of water next to agriculture. Much of this water is used but not consumed.

In hydroelectric plants, electricity is generated by sending water from behind dams into the blades of a turbine engine. When the turbine spins, it sends an electric current through attached wires. The current is channeled into a transformer and sent over power lines. In making electricity with water, the water actually remains at its source, and very little pollution occurs.

Groundwater is used to irrigate huge expanses of agricultural land in South Florida, a fact that is damaging the Everglades, one of the world's great wetlands.

FACT

Canada, the largest producer of hydroelectric power in the world, has over 600 large dams, as well as thousands of smaller ones. About half the major rivers of Canada (86 of 178) have been dammed for energy production, irrigation, flood control, or all three.

The usual alternative to making electricity with water is to burn fossil fuel, especially coal. The heat given off boils water, which produces steam. The steam is aimed at turbine

*Hoover Dam on the
Colorado River*

Hydroelectric Power

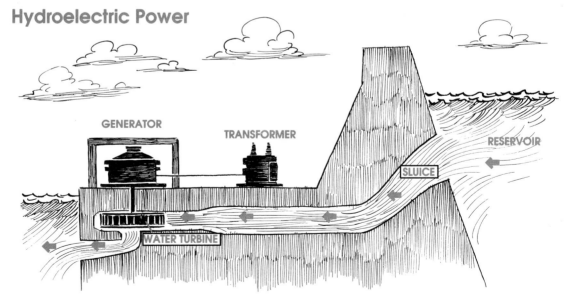

GENERATOR

TRANSFORMER

RESERVOIR

SLUICE

WATER TURBINE

blades to produce the electric current. Energy produced in this way is called thermal energy. These plants generally return the water to surface water sources, but it is usually much hotter than it was originally. This hot water raises the temperature of lakes and rivers, which can be very harmful to plant and animal life.

In nuclear power plants, electricity is produced by the energy released in nuclear reactions. A great deal of heat is also produced, and water is used to cool equipment and keep the process under control. Again, the water is likely to be hotter and it is also likely to be contaminated with radiation. While nuclear power plants do not create the air pollution associated with fossil-fuel burning plants, the problem of how to dispose of nuclear waste is very troubling.

Still another way that water can be used in the production of energy is in the generation of methane and biogas. These gases are produced by bacterial action on sludge from treated wastewater. Biogas can be used to run electric generators, and methane can be used for fuel. We will learn more about this in Chapter 5.

The production of energy and water issues are closely interrelated. Water is used in the production of energy. Energy is used to transport and treat water. Having enough of one resource is vital to having enough of the other.

Water in Making Products

Water is one of the most essential resources for many industries. It flows in huge volume through factories everywhere. It can be heated to create steam to run machinery and warm buildings. It can be used to cool hot metal (as in the production of steel) and to cool air. It is an important compo-

In this paper and wood-pulp mill, water containing waste is sent into a settling pond before it is discharged back into the watershed.

nent in many products, such as chemicals, pharmaceuticals (drugs, cosmetics, lotions, shampoos, etc.), and beverages. It is used to process food. It washes away waste in countless industrial processes, including the manufacture of paper.

The water used in some industries, such as food and beverage processing, must be absolutely clean and pure. Other industries, such as manufacturing plants that use water to operate machinery, may use a lower quality.

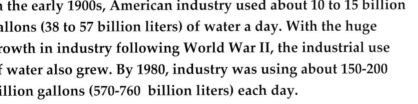

In the early 1900s, American industry used about 10 to 15 billion gallons (38 to 57 billion liters) of water a day. With the huge growth in industry following World War II, the industrial use of water also grew. By 1980, industry was using about 150-200 billion gallons (570-760 billion liters) each day.

FACT

It takes about 39,000 gallons (147,600 liters) of water to manufacture a single automobile. This may seem incredible, since an automobile is a hard, dry object. But water is used to produce the steel, glass, plastic, and fabric that make up the car. (It takes at least 30,000 gallons [114,000 liters] of water just to produce a ton of steel.) Water is also used in the assembly process, to heat and cool buildings and machinery, and to wash away wastes. And it takes water to run that automobile, too, even if it runs on gasoline. About 70 gallons (266 liters) of water are required to produce 1 gallon (3.8 liters) of gasoline from crude oil!

Water used by industry is usually returned to its source after use. But it is seldom returned in the same condition. At the very least, it is likely to be much warmer. And more often than not, it is loaded with contaminants. Water used in the paper industry, for example, is likely to contain nondegradable organic and chlorine-based substances.

Transportation

Native Americans used the surface waters of this continent for transportation for hundreds of years with little or no ecological impact. But with the coming of European settlers and the building of cities, dugout canoes gave way to barges, steamships, and even ocean-going vessels. The use of such ships on the Great Lakes and the Mississippi and Ohio rivers opened up the American continent. Shipping routes allowed furs and other natural resources to be brought out from the interior and timber for building to be moved where it was needed. These shipping lanes connected coal mines, steel mills, and factories. They enabled huge cities to grow.

But this growth has not been without cost. Using waterways for industrial shipping can be very damaging to the environment. The damage caused by shipping includes fuel spills, which coat the water with oil slicks and coal dust, and sulfur-laden fumes belched into the air from the smokestacks of ships and shoreline factories. In addition, shore-

lines are eroded by increased shipping and coastal areas are damaged by the building and maintenance of harbors.

For example, the Mississippi River has been dredged and straightened to accommodate barges carrying tons of coal, grain, and other commodities. Some 425 million tons (383 million metric tons) of commodities were carried along this river route in 1987. The Mississippi has been called the nation's north-south freight highway. But it has become so polluted as a result of all this traffic and the industries that have grown up along its shores that it has also been called the nation's longest sewer.

Another way that water is used for transportation is to carry solid materials, such as coal, through pipelines. One such pipeline extends 275 miles (443 kilometers) from the Black Mesa coal mine in Arizona to a power plant in Mojave, Nevada. Inside the pipe, crushed coal is suspended in an equal amount of water. This "slurry" moves fairly quickly through the pipeline. When the slurry reaches the power plant, the coal is separated from the water and used to generate electricity. The water is too polluted to dump into surface waters, so some is used in the cooling system of the power plant, and the rest is dumped into large open reservoirs and allowed to evaporate.

A series of locks and dams (right) were built on the Mississippi River so that ships (left) can travel upriver despite changes in elevation along the way. This ship is being loaded with grain which would otherwise have to be shipped overland to an ocean port.

51

But the water used in this pipeline is pumped from aquifers that lie beneath the reservations of the Hopi and Navajo Indians. The Hopis feel that robbing the Earth of the water is morally wrong. They are also concerned that such pumping may deplete the springs that provide drinking and farming water and may cause other environmental damage.

Using water to transport coal in pipelines makes sense only if water is considered cheap and plentiful, and if you don't mind that the by-product is severely polluted.

Fishing, Wildlife, and Fun

As long as people have lived near lakes and rivers they have relied on the water for food. Commercial fishing has been an important industry as well as a vital source for food around the world. But without care, any body of water— even an ocean—can be overfished.

And an even greater problem for commercial fishing is pollution. For example, fishing used to be one of the major industries in the Great Lakes. Now, pollution has killed off many species of fish and left most of the remainder unsafe to eat. Commercial fishing has nearly died out on the Great Lakes. Pollution has damaged commercial fishing in at least some of the lakes and rivers of virtually all the developed countries of the world.

FACT

In 1989, researchers studying fish taken from the Great Lakes found that 9 out of 10 were contaminated with toxic chemicals such as DDT and PCBs. About half were contaminated enough to be considered dangerous to humans.

Debris such as six-pack rings thrown into water can harm wildlife (left). Pleasure boating and waterskiing (right) can also be harmful to the plants and animals that live in the water.

Surface waters and wetland areas are home to a great many species of plants and animals other than fish. As these areas become threatened by pollution and other human activities, the plants and animals are threatened, too. And once a species becomes extinct, it is gone forever.

Water is also used for recreation—sports fishing, swimming, boating, and waterskiing. Most of us have enjoyed at least some of these activities, and it would sadden us to think of never being able to do any of them again.

But what if these "fun" things we do are hurting our environment? For example, motorboat propellers stir up sediment, and their wakes erode shorelines. Their engines pollute the water as well as the air. Careless disposal of trash can create serious hazards for other people and for animals.

We must all be more responsible about the way we use our waterways if we hope to continue enjoying them.

And after all is said and done, one of the most wonderful ways to enjoy a lake, a river, or a stream is simply to sit and look at it. But even this simple pleasure is threatened by our misuse of rivers, lakes, and wetlands.

Chapter 4

Pollution—
Making Our Water
Undrinkable

HUMAN LIFE DEPENDS on an adequate supply of clean water. The World Health Organization estimates that 80 percent of all illnesses are related to water. How clean is your water supply?

You probably know that the chemical makeup of water is H_2O—two hydrogen atoms bonded to an oxygen atom. But actually, there is almost no water as pure as that. Many kinds of substances, both natural and manufactured, attach to water molecules and contaminate them. Some of this contamination is not harmful, and some may even be beneficial. Some contamination is merely a nuisance, and some can be deadly poison.

In March 1990, the United States Centers for Disease Control reported that 26,000 cases of illness known to have been caused by contaminated drinking water occurred between 1986 and 1988. Thousands more were suspected but could not be proved.

FACT

Over 700 different chemicals have been found in drinking water across North America. Many of these substances have never been tested so no one knows whether they are harmful to humans. Of those that have been tested, 22 have been listed by the National Academy of Sciences as carcinogens (capable of causing cancer). Others are known to be harmful, though not necessarily carcinogenic.

Health officials have set standards for the upper limit of some of the chemicals known to be highly dangerous. Many others have not yet had standards set. It is important to set standards because water suppliers are required to monitor levels only of chemicals for which standards have been set. If no standard has been set for a chemical, water companies don't have to test for—or report—its presence.

Contaminants

Water contaminants are usually measured in parts per million or parts per billion. One part per million means one molecule of contaminant for every million molecules of water. Just how small is that? You can find out.

An Earth Experience

Parts Per Million

You will need nine small, clear plastic or glass containers. Number them from 1 to 9. Using a medicine dropper, place 10 drops of food coloring into the first container. Food coloring is already diluted to a ratio of 1:10—which means there is 1 part of dye for each 10 parts of water. Take 1 drop of food coloring from container #1 and place it in container #2. Add 9 drops of clean water to this container. You now have a solution with a ratio of 1:100, 1 part dye to 100 parts water. Now take 1 drop from container #2 and place it in container #3. Add 9 drops of water to this container. What is the ratio now? (1:1000) Continue this process, taking 1 drop from the previous container and adding 9 drops of clean water. When all nine containers have 10 drops of solution, figure the ratio for each one. Container #6 will have 1 part food coloring to 1 million parts water and container #9 will have 1 part per billion.

Microorganisms. Some contaminants are easily detected because they change the way water looks or smells. But even water that looks and smells fine can be polluted. One category of "invisible" contaminants is microorganisms, microscopic-sized plants and animals. There are three kinds of microorganisms that can be very dangerous in drinking water—bacteria, viruses, and protozoa. Throughout history, such microorganisms in drinking water have caused a great deal of sickness and death.

A hydrologist (water scientist) testing the quality of water from a well near a landfill that produces too much leachate.

In the spring of 1991, many Iraqi people suffered from waterborne disease in the aftermath of the Persian Gulf War. Devastating storms in Bangladesh in May 1991 also left thousands of people without safe drinking water, and the resulting outbreaks of illness added to the people's misery.

You may have smelled a funny odor in a swimming pool when chlorine has been added to keep the water safe for swimming. Since the early 1900s, many public water supplies, particularly in industrialized countries, have been treated with chlorine to kill bacteria. This has dramatically reduced such waterborne diseases as cholera and typhoid and has saved many, many lives. But chlorination is less effective against viruses and protozoa. Additional treatment processes are needed to kill these microorganisms.

Inorganic Compounds. Chemical compounds are classified as organic or inorganic. Organic compounds are carbon-based—they contain the element carbon (C). Virtually all

57

WATER POLLUTANTS

CATEGORY	EXAMPLES	WHY THEY ARE A PROBLEM	WHAT CAN BE DONE
MICRO-ORGANISMS	Bacteria Viruses Protozoa	Bacteria in water can cause diseases such as cholera and typhoid fever. Viruses in water can cause diseases, too, such as hepatitis A and polio. Protozoa are single-celled microscopic animals that can also cause diseases such as giardiosis.	Disinfection of water, usually with chlorine, will kill most bacteria. Additional water treatment procedures, such as coagulation, sedimentation, and filtration, can help to eliminate micro-organisms from water.
SUSPENDED SOLIDS	Feces Dirt Leaves	These materials can carry microorganisms into water supplies. They can also increase BOD (biochemical oxygen demand), leading to excessive algae growth.	Screens generally keep these materials out of water treatment plants. Tiny bits that enter can be removed as above by coagulation, sedimentation, and filtration.
INORGANIC COMPOUNDS	Minerals such as salt, iron, lead, mercury, copper, zinc, etc.	Some minerals in water are beneficial in small amounts. Excessive quantities can stain plumbing fixtures and give water a bad taste and smell. Lead and mercury are harmful to humans even in small amounts.	Reverse osmosis generally works to remove inorganic compounds from water.
SYNTHETIC ORGANIC COMPOUNDS	THMS (trihalomethanes) such as chloroform, formed when chlorine added to water reacts with other compounds. Trichloroethylene — a septic cleaner. Pesticides Gasoline	Many synthetic organic compounds are carcinogenic — capable of causing cancer.	Carbon filters are often used to remove synthetic organic chemicals from water.
RADIOACTIVE MATERIALS	Radon	Can cause cancer.	Removed with carbon filters.

This confined disposal facility in Ohio consists of dikes built to contain contaminated sediment. Because it looks safe and has no odor, birds are drawn to the water and people swim in it.

plant and animal life-forms are carbon-based. Inorganic compounds don't contain carbon. Minerals such as iron and lead are inorganic compounds.

Most naturally occurring inorganic contaminants are minerals found in soil that dissolve or become suspended in water. Few of these are harmful, and most can be beneficial in small quantities. "Mineral waters," containing calcium, magnesium, and potassium, and other minerals are very popular among many people. Other minerals may have unpleasant characteristics. For example, excessive iron can cause unsightly stains on bathroom fixtures and may give an unpleasant taste and odor to drinking water.

Another problem occurs when the minerals found in the Earth's surface accumulate in excessively large quantities in water. Sometimes these minerals can even be transformed into more harmful versions of themselves. These processes (excessive accumulation and transformation) can be accelerated by the phenomenon known as acid rain. Acid rain is precipitation that is contaminated with acidic substances, such as sulfuric and nitric acids, resulting from the burning of fossil fuels. When it falls on land, acid rain can release toxic minerals from the soil. These minerals find their way into surface water supplies, harming fish and plant life.

Acid rain and other air pollutants work together in harming trees and water systems.

The inorganic minerals of greatest concern include lead and mercury.

Lead is one of the most worrisome contaminants found in water. It cannot be detected by look, smell, or taste, but even a tiny bit can cause devastating health problems. It is most dangerous to unborn babies, infants, and small children. High-level exposure to lead can cause brain damage and death. But even low and moderate levels of exposure, over long periods of time, such as from regularly drinking water contaminated with lead, can cause nervous system damage in children. Hyperactivity and learning disabilities are two examples of such damage.

The removal of lead from most gasoline and a ban on the sale of lead-based paint have decreased exposure to lead in the United States. But Americans continue to export leaded gasoline to other parts of the world. Old water systems using lead pipes continue to be a serious source of lead in drinking water. Where drinking water is highly acidic or otherwise corrosive, it is more likely to contain elevated levels of lead.

In drinking water and food, mercury can lead to nerve and muscle disorders and death. Even an extremely small amount of mercury can be harmful, and many surface water systems have been polluted with mercury from industrial wastewater. As a result of changes in water chemistry after the construction of a huge dam near James Bay in Quebec, Canada, mercury in fish threatens the health of local Cree Indians, who eat a great deal of fish.

Nitrate is an inorganic chemical found in fertilizers. High nitrate levels cause problems primarily for infants. In a baby's body, nitrate is converted to nitrite, which keeps the blood from transporting oxygen and can lead to brain damage.

A sediment sample taken from Duluth Harbor in Minnesota is being tested for the presence of PCBs and heavy metals.

High nitrate levels in surface water and groundwater are usually the result of agricultural practices. Chemical fertilizers and animal wastes are high in nitrogen, which is converted to nitrate in the soil. This nitrate works its way down through soil to groundwater sources. Rainfall runoff washes nitrate into surface waters. Septic tank leaks also contribute to nitrogen in the soil and groundwater.

Organic Compounds

Organic compounds that contaminate drinking water, are also both naturally occurring and synthetic.

Compounds Nature Didn't Make. Prior to World War II, most of the products used in homes and industry were based on natural components. Since the late 1940s, there has

The Grand Calumet River flows into Lake Michigan near oil storage tanks and steel mills. The river has become a toxic hot spot because of the contaminants in the water.

been a great increase in the number and uses of synthetic (manufactured) materials. These materials are made of chemicals not found in nature. Often they are produced by subjecting petroleum and petroleum by-products to various chemical processes. Many do not readily break down when disposed of, and they can be dangerous to plants, animals, and people. These carbon-based chemicals range from weedkillers to polystyrene (as in Styrofoam cups), from life-saving medicines to refrigerator coolant.

Organic chemicals found in drinking water include trichloroethylene (a compound used in insecticides), tetrachloroethylene (a solvent), vinyl chloride (a plastic), carbon tetrachloride (a solvent formerly used to clean clothing), chloroform (an anesthetic), and aldicarb (a pesticide). Benzene, from which numerous other solvents, plastics, and insecticides are made, is known to cause leukemia (cancer of the blood) after long exposure.

In the early 1970s, researchers discovered that a group of organic chemicals called THMs (trihalomethanes) were created when water was treated with chlorine—the most common method of killing microorganisms in water. It seems that chlorine interacts with other compounds commonly found in water, creating these new compounds. THMs are believed to be carcinogens. Chloroform, the most commonly found THM, is used in refrigerants and anesthetics. Chlorobenzene is another THM used in the production of insecticides and dyes. Inside the body it appears to act as a depressant to the central nervous system.

Bromoform (tribromomethane) is a THM used to dissolve wax and oil and in creating fire-resistant chemicals. It was never intended for consumption. But it is sometimes formed in water that has been chlorinated. All these THMs have been linked to cancer in laboratory tests.

Radiation. Radiation is the flow of atomic and subatomic particles and waves. There has always been radioactivity in the environment, but this "background radiation" is considered to have little impact on human health. However, our increased use of nuclear materials for energy production, weapons systems, and medical use, has greatly increased the amount of radiation in our environment. And the potential for radiation contamination of drinking water has thus increased, too.

Drinking water contaminated with radiation is extremely dangerous to human beings. It can lead to all the problems associated with radiation sickness, including nausea, headache,

This solid-waste burial ground is used to dispose of low-level radioactive waste. Such sites must be maintained carefully to be sure that the buried drums do not leak the waste into the groundwater.

63

loss of hair, cancer and other illnesses, and death. Many people in eastern Europe and the Soviet Union suffer from various illnesses as a result of drinking water contaminated with radiation by the Chernobyl nuclear power plant accident of 1986.

Even without such human-caused disasters, radiation can be a problem with water. Radium, a highly radioactive metallic element, is present in many types of rock. When radium decays, it gives off radon, a radioactive gas. Radon can seep into buildings through cracks in the foundation, walls, and floors. It can also enter a home through its water supply. Radon is thought to cause lung cancer.

When a massive chemical spill into the Rhine River occurred in 1986, residents of the village of Unkel had to collect water from fire-department tanks in order to have drinkable water.

The Sources of Contamination

So how do all these strange and horrible things get into our water? The vast majority of contaminants are a result of the things that people do.

The two basic categories for describing the sources of water pollution are *point* and *nonpoint* sources. Point sources of pollution are specific sites where contamination is known to occur. A factory discharging waste-water into a river is a point source of pollution. Nonpoint sources are more widespread and general. For example, farmland rainwater runoff, contaminated with fertilizers and pesticides, seeps into groundwater and flows into surface waters.

Of course, the differences between point and nonpoint sources sometimes are blurred,

When homeowners who live on a lake or river use too much fertilizer, the water frequently becomes choked with unwanted plants. In the past this has usually been corrected by using poisonous herbicides. This aquatic harvesting machine can safely remove the excess growth without harming the water quality.

and it is not always possible to keep everything in nice, neat categories.

Dumping into a Lake or River. Direct discharge occurs when a factory discharges its dirty water directly into a lake or river. This type of pollution is the most heavily regulated today. Anyone discharging water into a lake or river must have a permit from the EPA. This regulation has helped revive a number of seriously polluted surface waters, but a great deal of dumping, legal and illegal, continues. Many people think stricter requirements are needed.

Accidents. In 1986, the city of Farmington, New Mexico, installed two underground gasoline storage tanks and filled them with gasoline. Overnight, thousands of gallons of gasoline disappeared. Fearing that thieves were siphoning out the gasoline, officials put a fence around the tanks and filled them again. When that gaso-

Sources of Water Contamination

Point Sources

Direct discharge
Accidents
Deep-well injection
Leaky landfills
Leaking underground
storage tanks
Abandoned hazardous-
waste sites
Septic tanks

Nonpoint Sources

Agricultural runoff
Urban runoff
Mining, logging, grazing

Gasoline spills every day. The poisonous liquid is often allowed to just soak into the ground, where it can make the groundwater useless for drinking. This spill is being cleaned up by removing the contaminated soil.

line disappeared, too, they finally realized that the contractor who had installed the tanks had forgotten to put plugs in the bottom. Twenty thousand gallons (76,000 liters) of gasoline had literally been poured into the soil and was heading for the water table. Close to $1 million was spent to clean up the mess before it ruined the city's water supply.

This is just one example of an accident that threatened to pollute water. There have been hundreds more which have cost billions of dollars to clean up. And many are not discovered until after a water source is permanently damaged.

Leaking Landfills. Millions of tons of trash are dumped in landfills (specially constructed garbage dumps) all across North America. For most of us, it is out of sight and out of mind. But all too often, our trash comes back to haunt us in the form of leachate.

Leachate is the liquid that seeps from landfills. It consists of rainwater that has mixed with all the substances buried in a landfill. It contains many, many dissolved contaminants.

This contaminated water flows from landfills and seeps down through the soil to groundwater. Most landfills built before the 1980s were poorly lined, or not lined at all, and there is nothing to keep leachate from reaching the ground-water. These poorly built and improperly maintained land-fills are major sources of groundwater contamination.

Even the best landfills are not 100 percent free of leaks. Leachate may run out, contaminating nearby water.

Today's landfills are built more carefully, with drainage tiles and wells for testing leachate. But leaky landfills remain a serious threat to the water that lies under them.

We need strict codes for landfill construction, but we also can all do our part by reducing the amount of trash we send to landfills. We must reuse and recycle as much trash as possible and be very careful of how we dispose of hazardous waste. Never throw household chemicals into the trash or dump them down a toilet. Save them for a Clean Sweep Day in your town.

According to the EPA, some 90 billion gallons (342 billion liters) of contaminated water seep from 18,500 municipal landfills in the United States each year. Most of this contaminated water finds its way into surface or groundwater sources.

FACT

Landfills and Leachate

You will need a medium-sized cardboard box. Cut away part of the front of the box so that you can see what is happening inside. Line the bottom with aluminum foil. Place sand in the box so that it is higher on both sides than in the middle. Place a small bowl or saucer partially filled with water in the center of the box. This is a "lake" in the "valley." The top of one of the slopes is your "landfill" site.

Between the landfill and the lake, place a sheet of aluminum foil so that leachate will be directed from the landfill to the lake. Cover the foil with sand, making sure that the edge of the foil overlaps the edge of the lake. Place a few bits of paper or cloth that have been soaked with red food coloring into your landfill. Now pour a glass of water over your landfill, simulating rain. Within a short time, the red dye should begin to leach into your lake.

Deep Well Injection. When concern about polluted surface waters arose in the late 1950s, many industries began looking into sub-surface ways to dispose of liquid wastes contaminated with all kinds of toxic chemicals. Deep wells were dug so that liquid waste could be pumped deep into the Earth, to a porous area sealed off from the aquifers above by a layer of impermeable rock. It sounds good in theory, but what happens in practice is that impermeable layers of rock sometimes develop cracks that allow the hazardous materials to infiltrate drinking-water aquifers.

Another problem with deep well injection is that some of these chemical wastes are so corrosive that they eat through the impermeable rock, destroying the barrier that keeps them "safely" disposed of.

And sometimes the lining of the well leaks, allowing the toxic contents to seep into the soil around it, and thus into groundwater supplies. It is estimated that about 10 billion gallons (38 billion liters) of liquid hazardous waste is disposed of by deep well injection in the United States each year.

Both the chemical and petroleum industries are heavy users of deep well injection. Many such wells are located in the Great Lakes area as well as in Texas and Louisiana, but they can also be found in many other parts of the United States.

Leaking Underground Storage Tanks. During the 1950s, large metal storage tanks were buried underground. Many contained gasoline, while others were used to store various toxic chemicals. Most of these tanks were expected to last about thirty years. Those thirty years are now up, and many of the tanks are corroded and rusty, and they are silently spilling their toxic contents into the ground.

The EPA believes that gasoline leaking from underground storage

Storage tanks that were put underground as a fire-safety measure have begun to corrode and leak, creating a new set of problems for our land and water.

tanks is a very serious threat to groundwater. According to the EPA, some 11 million gallons (42 million liters) of gasoline seep into groundwater resources each year. They estimate that there are 800,000 corroded steel storage tanks buried under old gasoline stations, farms, and other businesses across the country. Gasoline contains benzene and EDP, both chemicals suspected of causing cancer, and a number of other toxic substances as well.

It takes only a small amount of gasoline in water to make it undrinkable. How much would you like in your water?

Hazardous-Waste Sites. The boom in manufacturing and industry following World War II led to a huge increase in industrial waste, much of which is highly toxic. While everyone enjoyed the prosperity of the 1950s and 1960s, as well as the wonderful new modern products that were available, few people seemed to care about how this waste was dis-

For generations it was regarded as enough to put hazardous materials in storage drums before disposing of them. But, like underground storage tanks, the drums eventually corrode, poisoning the landscape and our water supplies.

posed of. Numerous 55-gallon (209-liter) drums of poison were hastily buried in shallow graves or dumped into wetland areas. Like the underground storage tanks, many of these hazardous-waste containers all across the country are now leaking.

Leaking Septic Systems. Many households outside of towns use septic systems to dispose of their sewage. When toilets are flushed and showers are run, septic systems send the waste first into a tank where the solid matter settles and then direct the liquid into an underground area, called the septic field, set aside for this purpose. The water then trickles down through the soil of the field and back into the groundwater. By the time it reaches the water table, the water is supposed to be clean enough to use again.

Septic tanks are a great threat to groundwater resources, not only because of the human waste discharged from them, but also because chemicals are added to clean or "degrease" them. Bacteria and chemicals can contaminate groundwater when the septic tank is located too near the water supply, or when the water table rises during heavy rainfall. Thus, the drinking water in areas with many septic systems is frequently polluted with the trichloroethylene used to degrease septic tanks.

Poison Runoff — Nonpoint Pollution

Water pollution that does not have a specific source— nonpoint pollution—may be more easily thought of as poison runoff. Such runoff causes at least half the problems affecting surface-water quality in the United States. Nonpoint sources of pollution include farmland runoff, urban runoff, and runoff from mining, forestry, and construction activities.

This form of pollution can cause fish to become starved for oxygen because excess bacteria and algae use up the oxygen in the water. The toxins in runoff can make fish diseased, and the fish, in turn, can harm people who eat them.

FACT

Of 17,000 rivers, lakes, and streams listed by the EPA as seriously degraded (damaged), only 4 percent were damaged largely by direct discharge from sewage plants and factories. The rest were being degraded mostly by runoff.

Runoff from Farms. Because farmers apply many pesticides to their fields, runoff can carry these toxic substances into our waterways. Farmland runoff also carries large quantities of soil (which settles to the bottom of lakes and rivers as sediment), soil nutrients, and bacteria into surface waters. This material is high in biochemical oxygen demand (BOD), which promotes algae growth and depletes waterways of oxygen.

Runoff from Cities. We often think of rainstorms as nature's way of freshening the air. But with all the pollution

An urban lake in Madison, Wisconsin, being tested for the quality of the water, which can be harmed by runoff from city streets after a heavy rainfall.

in the air and on the land, even the most gentle summer shower can be a vehicle for water pollution.

In cities and towns across North America, rainwater runs across lawns and driveways, construction sites, and parking lots. It runs down streets and into sewers. Along the way it picks up all kinds of chemicals—from the zinc, copper, and lead in auto and industrial emissions to weed and insect killers such as 2,4-D and diazinon. It also picks up bacteria from animal and food waste, salt from road de-icing, and soil eroded from construction sites.

After this water disappears into a storm sewer, what then? It may flow directly into local surface waters, where its chemical contaminants can harm fish and plant life. It can also make the water undesirable for recreational uses, not to mention dangerous for drinking.

If we're lucky, it flows to a sewage-treatment plant along with human sewage flushed down toilets and washed down drains all over the city. But if the sewage system can't handle the double load of storm water and sewage, both types of water may be dumped directly into nearby lakes. And even if the polluted water reaches the sewage-treatment plant, the plant probably can't handle such a varied concoction of pollutants.

Sewer overflow after a heavy rain can be harmful to the wastewater treatment process in a city. Many cities are now building major tunnels and reservoirs to handle the overflow.

Saltwater Infiltration. Saltwater from the sea can flow into freshwater sources. Called saltwater infiltration, this happens when too much water is taken from a freshwater aquifer near the ocean, allowing salt water from the ocean to infiltrate the aquifer. Salt water is a threat to aquifers used by people all along the Atlantic and Gulf of Mexico coasts.

Infiltration is currently a serious problem for the people of Long Island, New York. As urbanization spreads, rainwater is more likely to be directed to Long Island Sound or the Atlantic Ocean instead of reaching the aquifer through the soil. At the same time, aquifers are being depleted by increased use. Unless the balance between inflow and outflow is restored, these aquifers will soon become too salty to use.

Polluted Rivers

Although the Cuyahoga River is a famous example of a polluted river, the United States is not alone in the problem of water pollution.

The Danube River flows through or along eight European countries. Its watershed is populated by 80 million people. It has played an important role in history, literature, and art. And it is crippled by pollution. From its headwaters

As rivers worldwide become polluted, cities such as Bogota, Colombia (left), are having to construct water systems that will provide clean water for their citizens. Many cities, such as this one in Poland (right), continue to discharge pollutants into urban water sources. This plant makes fertilizer and discharges its waste into the Vistula River.

in Germany's Black Forest to its mouth on the Black Sea, it is the recipient of huge quantities of human sewage, farmland runoff, and industrial discharge.

About one-fifth of the world's chemicals are produced along the banks of the Rhine River in Germany. Many of the same millions who use it as a drinking-water source also use it as their sewage outlet.

After passing through Poland's Silesian industrial district and the city of Krakow, the Vistula River is so polluted that it cannot be used for irrigation because it kills microbes in the soil and withers plants. Nor can it be used by industry because it corrodes pipes and machinery.

And many poor countries of the Third World also suffer from water pollution. As they struggle to improve their economies, their pollution problems are increasing as well.

What's Being Done

The U.S. federal government has passed a number of laws to try to control and clean up water pollution.

In 1972 Congress passed a group of amendments to the Federal Water Pollution Control Act of 1956. These amendments became known as the Clean Water Act. The goal of the act was to restore and then maintain the purity of our nation's waterways. This act in turn has been amended (most notably with the Water Quality Act of 1987) several times as Congress calls for stricter regulations on polluters.

The Safe Drinking Water Act of 1974 established policies for protecting drinking-water sources.

The Resource Conservation and Recovery Act of 1976 was passed to prevent future problems with hazardous-waste dumping. But actually following through with the requirements of these laws is expensive and difficult, and the new law had little effect on hazardous-waste dumps already in existence.

To deal with this problem, the Comprehensive Environmental Response, Compensation, and Liability Act, also called the "Superfund," was passed in 1980. This bill attempts to hold polluters responsible for the messes they create. It also set up a fund to provide money for the cleanup of high priority sites where no private party could be held responsible.

So the legislation is in place. What we need now is stricter enforcement. Too often safety standards are exceeded without penalty. Deadlines pass unmet. And we haggle over who is to pay.

The Congressional Budget Office suggests steep taxes for companies that create and dispose of hazardous waste. But all too often the polluter cannot be found. Then innocent people get hurt both by the pollution itself and by the cost of cleaning it up.

Industry Working to Prevent Pollution

Not all businesses are guilty of polluting the environment. Many are actually involved in cleaning up their acts.

Since the 1970s, the 3M Company (Minnesota Mining and Manufacturing) has promoted the "3 P Plus" program—the idea that "pollution prevention pays." In 1984 this progressive company made some alterations in its sandpaper-making process, which reduced the amount of hazardous waste generated and, incidentally, saved the company money. The company continues to encourage its employees to think of ways to eliminate polluting wastes.

The United States Steel Corporation (now called USX) is another company working to reduce its hazardous waste. It found a way to mix sludge from plants that turned coal into coke, formerly a hazardous-waste problem, with other solid metals to create a fuel that could be used for energy. It turned waste into useful products.

Motivated by increased costs of treating wastewater and disposing of waste, many industries are looking for ways to conserve and protect water. We need to encourage more companies to find ways to reuse their toxic materials rather than dumping them. This would be a big help to water-pollution problems.

The billions of dollars spent in the 1970s and 1980s on cleaning up pollution have, in many cases, given us less dirty water. But still these waters are not completely clean. Some of the rivers that were unable to support fish in past decades now have a few species of hardy fish in them. But in many cases, the fish are still not safe to eat.

We have a long way to go before everyone's water is always pollution-free.

Chapter 5

Making Water Safe

NOT FOR MANY YEARS has it been safe for a person to go to the average lake or river and drink out of it. All water has to be treated in some way to make it safe to drink. Water treatment includes all the ways we change the chemical makeup of water. This includes purification of the water that comes into our homes, as well as removal of toxins from the wastewater that leaves it. It also includes desalination (the removal of salt from water) and water softening (the addition of salt to neutralize other minerals). The study of water treatment is a fascinating story about how people try to make "clean" water.

In ancient times, people knew that filtering water through sand could remove some impurities. But water treatment did not become widespread until the discovery of bacteria-killing chemicals in the late 1800s.

In the meantime, people continued to die from water-borne diseases, particularly typhoid fever and cholera. Both are very infectious diseases caused by bacteria. Cholera especially still breaks out in countries that are subject to great flooding, when sewage mixes with drinking-water sources. Hundreds of people may die from diseases.

About 15 percent of the American population get their drinking water from their own private wells. Their water gets no treatment unless the homeowner chooses to use some sort of in-home treatment system.

The other 85 percent of the American people get their drinking water from public supplies. Numerous laws regulate the water that comes from public supplies, including monitoring for some 83 toxic chemicals. However, many of the standards are regularly exceeded without prosecution, and many more toxins are not regulated.

The U.S. Council on Environmental Quality published a list of 33 toxic organic compounds that had been found in drinking water. They ranged from concentrations of a few parts per billion to 27,300 parts per billion of trichloroethylene found in a well in Pennsylvania.

Most American cities—about 75 percent—now get their drinking water from groundwater sources. Regardless of whether it comes from ground or surface water sources, it is usually treated in some way before it is distributed to homes and businesses.

Most of us assume that when we turn on a water faucet what comes out will be pure and safe to drink. But we must all make it our business to be sure that that assumption remains true.

Drinking-Water Treatment

As water is pumped into a treatment plant, large objects such as fish, sticks, and leaves are screened out. The water then moves into a tank where chemicals may be added.

Filtering Water

You will need 2 clear glass jars. In one jar , put some "muddy water," a solution of water and dirt. Set aside.

Fill a funnel with a layer of small pebbles, a layer of gravel, and a fairly thick layer of sand. Place the funnel in the mouth of the second jar. Pour a little clean water into this funnel to allow the layers of filtering material to pack together. Then slowly pour the muddy water into the funnel. If your filter is working correctly, you will see cleaner water flow into the jar beneath the funnel.

The minimal treatment for municipal supplies is the addition of chlorine to kill bacteria. Some cities are finding that by waiting to add chlorine until the end of the treatment process, they reduce the amount of THMs produced. Alum may also be added to help form "flocs," globs of sediment that settle at the bottom of the tank. Lime is sometimes added to neutralize acidity.

Mechanical mixers stir these chemicals into the water, which is then sent to a tank where large particles of impurities settle out.

Next, the water is filtered through sand to remove additional impurities. It may be aerated, which usually involves spraying it in the air to add oxygen. Aeration can make water smell and taste better. Chlorine is added to kill any remaining bacteria.

Fluoride may also be added. Small amounts of fluoride in water help prevent tooth decay. But too much dissolves tooth enamel, and new studies are linking fluoride to cancer. The addition of fluoride to drinking water remains a controversial issue.

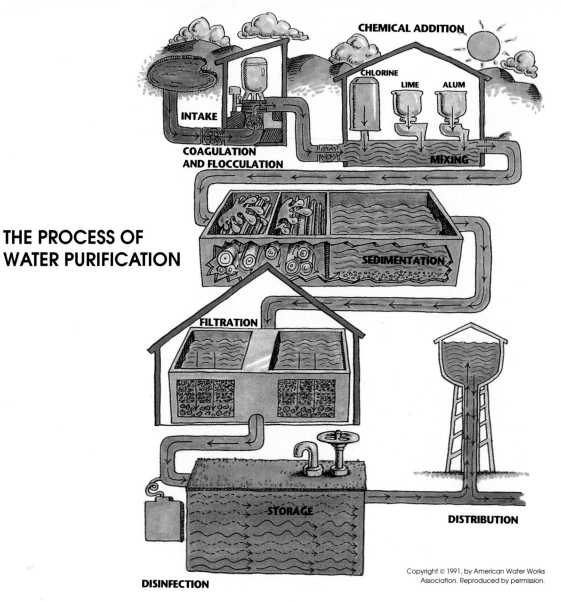

THE PROCESS OF WATER PURIFICATION

CHEMICAL ADDITION

CHLORINE

LIME

ALUM

INTAKE

COAGULATION AND FLOCCULATION

MIXING

SEDIMENTATION

FILTRATION

STORAGE

DISTRIBUTION

DISINFECTION

The treated water is then stored in an elevated tank or reservoir until distributed through water mains and into the pipes leading to homes and businesses.

Investigators have found hundreds of different chemicals in various water-treatment and distribution systems across the country, including asbestos. Some of these are additives—substances added during the treatment process.

Others are chemicals and minerals picked up when the water flows through pipes in the distribution system. Some of these can be quite harmful to humans.

Contamination of water in the distribution system is a major problem for water suppliers. Water may leave the treatment plant in drinkable condition but be contaminated by leaks in the system or by the pipes carrying the water.

Many American cities pump 40 to 50 percent more water through their systems than they can account for in billing. A staggering amount of water is lost through leaky pipes and breaks in the water main.

FACT

Sewage lines have been known to leak into or back up into water distribution systems. Thus drinking water is contaminated with sewage on its way to consumers.

Sometimes pipes are lined with asbestos, which may contaminate the water, or they may contain copper or lead, which can leach into drinking water, especially if the water is corrosive. All these metals have been found to be hazardous to human health.

Ensuring that quality water comes from all public water systems is no easy task.

Testing Your Drinking Water

If you get your drinking water from a private well, you should have it tested regularly to make sure that it has not become polluted. Your state or local health department can tell you how to have this done.

If you get your water from a public supply, you can ask your local water utility for a municipal supply analysis. This should tell you what they test for, the levels found, and the EPA limit. If you are still not satisfied, you can call your state or municipal health department to find out where to have your water tested. Or write to one of the following private labs for a testing kit, which can cost anywhere from $89 to $150 and up: National Testing Laboratories, 6151 Wilson Mills Rd., Cleveland, OH 44143, or Suburban Water Testing Laboratories, 4600 Kutztown Rd., Temple, PA 19560.

Many people drink bottled water because of their concern about drinking-water quality. Many water bottlers belong to the American Bottled Water Association, which has established regulations for its members. But these regulations are no more strict than the regulations that govern public water supplies. And many of the contaminants found in municipal drinking water are also found in bottled water.

Many people have their drinking water delivered to their homes in bottles. But they still need to be certain that it is clean and pure.

POLLUTANTS TO WATCH FOR IN DRINKING WATER	
LEAD	If your home has lead pipes, or lead solder in copper pipes, you risk having lead in your drinking water. It is now illegal to use lead in drinking-water pipes, but it may be present in older homes.
THMs	The most common THM is chloroform, which causes cancer in lab animals. You are most likely to be exposed to THMs if your water comes from a surface water source where organic matter mixes with chlorine.
NITRATES	These are most often found in agricultural areas. They are extremely dangerous for infants.
RADON	Radon is a naturally occurring radioactive gas. It is not likely to be a problem if your water comes from surface water.
VOCs *volatile organic compounds*	VOCs leach into groundwater from landfills and hazardous-waste dumps. They are chemicals used as degreasers and in dry cleaning, spot removers, air fresheners, and food processing, etc. They have been linked to cancer and other illnesses.
PESTICIDES	Pesticides, such as aldicarb, are most often found in drinking water in agricultural areas.

In-Home Treatment

Many people have decided that the solution to water-quality concerns is to treat their drinking water at home. There are several ways to do this.

Carbon Filters. Carbon (usually in the form of grains of charcoal that have been "activated"—specially treated to make them more absorbent) attracts contaminants such as organic chemicals like chloroform as the water flows through the tap. Carbon filters extract THMs, VOCs, radon, and pesticides. But they do nothing for lead, other metals, and nitrates.

Faucet-mounted filters are generally ineffective, because they have such a small amount of carbon. If you are going to use a carbon filter, it is better to use a countertop or under-sink model. You must still be sure to change the filters every couple of months.

Reverse Osmosis. This process removes inorganic contaminants, such as salts, nitrate, fluoride, iron, and lead. It consists of a special membrane—which acts as a sediment filter—that withdraws certain kinds of particles from the water, a storage tank, and a carbon filter. One of the main drawbacks of reverse osmosis units is that they tend to be water wasters.

Water Softeners. Salts and other minerals in water affect its taste and determine whether it is hard or soft.

In hard water, the presence of calcium and magnesium interferes with soap's ability to lather and rinse away, and hard water leaves a residue in kettles.

Small amounts of natural salts and minerals in water can make it taste good. Too much can be dangerous.

The common household water softener exchanges the calcium and magnesium found in hard water for sodium. In this way, the mineral content of water is reduced—it is made soft.

Making Ocean Water Drinkable

Desalination (also called desalinization) is the process by which salt and water are separated, leaving drinkable fresh water. Many Middle Eastern nations such as Israel, Egypt, and Saudi Arabia use desalination to increase their water supplies. A growing number of coastal industries in the United States consider desalination as the answer to their pure water needs. Polymetrics of Sunnyvale, California, is a company that provides desalinated water to companies that produce computer chips in Silicon Valley.

A solar still is a device that employs some of the same

processes that occur naturally in the hydrologic cycle (evaporation and condensation). It uses the energy of the sun to evaporate salty water into water vapor, leaving the salt behind. The desalted water condenses on tilted glass panels, and the condensed water filters into troughs, from which it is collected for use.

A solar still is a fairly simple way to desalt a small amount of water at a time. The process of distillation can be speeded up in large desalination plants that substitute other forms of energy for the sun. A number of different processes are used in such plants, but they all require a great deal of energy, which makes them very, very expensive. For this reason, it is still not practical to desalt the waters of the oceans in most parts of the world. Research is being conducted to make desalination technology less costly and more efficient.

Wastewater Treatment

We've looked at all the ways water is treated before it is used in homes. Just as important is wastewater treatment—the things that are done to water *after* it is used.

If you get your water from a surface water source, there's

This special equipment uses solar power to detoxify liquid hazardous waste. Particles of sunlight, called photons, break organic contaminants in liquid such as dioxins and PCBs into safer compounds.

87

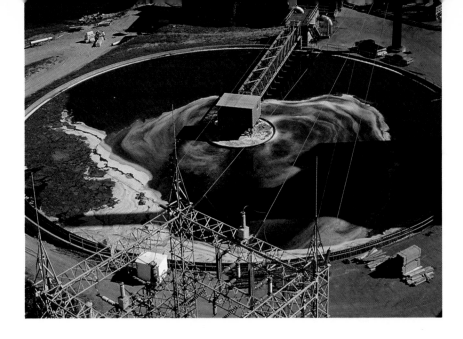

Many industries that use a lot of water pretreat wastewater before sending it to a water treatment plant. This water from a paper plant is being cleaned to remove most of the contaminants before it is released.

a good chance that your drinking water was once someone else's wastewater. That may sound awful, but most modern countries have systems that clean wastewater before it is returned to rivers. And remember, all the water on the planet is the same water that has been here for millions of years—all our water is recycled water.

Cleaning wastewater before returning it to a surface water source is what wastewater treatment, also called sewage treatment, is all about.

Wastewater treatment plants put water through the same purification processes that take place naturally in rivers and lakes. When a small quantity of waste enters a body of water, bacteria are attracted to it. The bacteria consume the waste, changing it to nutrients and carbon dioxide. The nutrient materials usually settle to the bottom.

During this process, the bacteria use up oxygen. When large quantities of waste enter the water, bacteria consume so much oxygen that there is none left for fish, which become oxygen-starved. If the waste contains certain nutrients that encourage plant growth, excessive quantities of small plants called algae grow. Such a situation is called algal bloom. Although these plants give off oxygen while alive, large quantities of oxygen are consumed when they die and decompose, further contributing to oxygen depletion. This process is called eutrophication.

Much more wastewater is now produced than surface water supplies can purify naturally. Wastewater treatment plants are built to assist natural processes and speed them along. Bacteria and other microorganisms are used to consume wastes without fear of using up all the oxygen because more can be added in the process. When the water is considered clean, it is returned to a nearby lake or river.

An important part of wastewater treatment is the removal of the solid material that bacteria in rivers and lakes would be attracted to and consume, thus using up oxygen. This need of bacteria to use up oxygen is called the biochemical oxygen demand (BOD) factor. Wastewater treatment facilities reduce the biochemical oxygen demand of the water they return to streams and lakes to avoid harming those bodies of water. They must also kill bacteria that can make people sick. Effluent (the water discharged from treat-

The purification of wastewater by bacteria can be speeded up by mixing it so that extra oxygen gets into the water.

ment plants) is tested to make sure that it meets BOD and harmful bacteria standards.

But there may still be pollutants in wastewater effluent even when the BOD is low. Some substances in wastewater cannot be consumed by bacteria or otherwise removed from wastewater. These substances include fertilizers, pesticides, and many kinds of other chemicals. A great deal of research is being done to improve wastewater treatment processes to eliminate these chemicals from effluent.

So, wastewater treatment is designed to: 1) lower BOD, 2) kill harmful bacteria, and 3) eliminate other harmful substances as much as possible.

Wastewater includes not only the sewage coming from homes but also from businesses and industries and storm-water runoff. Whether wastewater is flushed down a toilet, dumped down the drain of a beauty-parlor sink, washed down a gas-station drain, or poured into the sewer at the end of the block, it all ends up at the treatment plant.

Wastewater flow from homes and businesses is carried to the wastewater treatment plant by pipes and sewers. Sometimes there are separate systems for residential and industrial sewage and for storm-water runoff.

A Trip Through a Wastewater Treatment Plant

Wastewater treatment is usually discussed in terms of primary and secondary treatment. *Primary treatment* physically removes suspended (floating) solids from wastewater. *Secondary treatment* uses biological processes to remove contaminants dissolved in the water. At the end of secondary treatment, chemicals may be added to disinfect or further treat the water.

A wastewater treatment facility may look like any factory from the outside, but its job is a vital one of making sure that used water is returned to its source in good condition.

As wastewater enters the treatment plant, it goes through large, strong screens that keep floating objects such as sticks, leaves, rags, and pieces of garbage, from entering the treatment plant.

As the screened water enters the treatment plant, two things may happen. It may enter a mixing tank where chemicals can be added to start the cleaning-up process. These chemicals often include chlorine (which kills bacteria that make people sick), alum (which attaches to small particles in the water and drags them to the bottom), carbon (which gets rid of bad-smelling particles in the water), and lime (which makes water less acidic).

A treatment plant that does not add chemicals at this point may move the water through a grit chamber, which will slow it down just a little so that sand and gravel, otherwise known as "grit," settle out. Accumulated grit will usually be washed and landfilled.

Next, the wastewater will enter a sedimentation or holding tank. Here the water sits for a few hours, allowing solid particles to settle to the bottom or to float to the top. These solids, called primary sludge, are scraped from the bottom of the tank or skimmed from the top and sent to the digestion tank. The water now moves into secondary treatment.

Settling Tank

Fill a clear glass jar about two-thirds full of water. Add a spoonful of soil to the jar and mix well. Then let the jar sit for a few moments. Much of the soil should settle to the bottom of the jar. This is what happens in a settling tank, one of the most basic steps in wastewater treatment.

Using another jar, add the same amount of water and soil. This time, also add a teaspoon of alum (available in the spice section of a grocery store). Mix and then let it sit. What difference does the alum make?

Sludge

During both primary and secondary treatment, materials are removed from wastewater. This accumulated solid material is called sludge.

First the sludge is digested by bacteria, which reduces odor. Then it is dewatered, or dried, which reduces it in volume. Raw wastewater is generally over 99 percent water, less than 1 percent solid. Settled sludge may be about 3 percent solid. Additional processes to remove water from the sludge can bring it up to 20 percent solid (the consistency of wet mud) and 50 percent solid (the consistency of dry soil). At this point it can be disposed of (landfilled, incinerated and then landfilled, or dumped in the ocean), or added to soil as a fertilizer, depending on its chemical makeup.

Many people are becoming concerned over the effects of dumping sewage and sludge in the oceans. We used to think oceans were big enough to handle anything. But it's not true.

On land, however, sludge can have some benefit. It im-

WASTEWATER TREATMENT

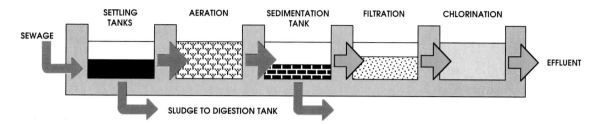

SEWAGE | SETTLING TANKS | AERATION | SEDIMENTATION TANK | FILTRATION | CHLORINATION | EFFLUENT

SLUDGE TO DIGESTION TANK

proves water retention, keeps soil soft, slows erosion, and replaces nutrients. Sludge has been used to revitalize land spoiled by strip mines and industry. After being treated with sludge, these barren sites can be planted with grass and shrubs.

Secondary Treatment

During secondary treatment, microorganisms are given prime working conditions to break down any waste that remains in the water. One secondary treatment is called the activated sludge process. The sludge is aerated and allowed to settle to simulate natural biological functions.

In one tank, wastewater, microorganisms, and oxygen are mixed together. This is called aeration. After the microorganisms have been given time to munch on and digest the wastewater, the wastewater moves to a sedimentation tank where solids are again given a chance to settle out. Some of what settles out is the "activated sludge," which is rich in microorganisms and will be used again on the next batch of wastewater. The rest is secondary sludge, which, like primary sludge, gets sent to a digestion tank.

Some municipalities make fertilizer from their sludge. This works only if the sewage is toxin-free. In Milwaukee, Wisconsin, specially treated sewage sludge becomes Milorganite, a high-quality fertilizer.

After treatment, the water is tested to make sure that it meets effluent standards. Finally it is dumped into its source, from which it may soon be brought back into use as fresh water.

Another form of secondary treatment is trickling filters. In this process the water moves through layers of different types of filters. These filters may be beds of charcoal, gravel, sand, or other loosely packed materials. As the water passes through these filters, microorganisms work on suspended and dissolved contaminants.

A sanitation lagoon is most like nature, the only difference being that the cleansing process takes place in surface water set aside for this purpose rather than in a multiple-use lake or stream. In this process, sunlight, algae, and oxygen interact to digest the waste in wastewater. This slow process may be speeded up by adding oxygen to the water.

After secondary treatment, the wastewater is usually subjected to the process of disinfection. Chlorine is added to kill any harmful bacteria that may remain.

FACT

When a system being built at Boston Harbor is ready, treated wastewater from Boston's toilets will be dumped 10 miles (16 kilometers) out, 400 feet (120 meters) deep in the Atlantic Ocean. It is being called "the longest flush in the world."

Treating Water from Industry

Industrial wastewater can cause special problems for sewage treatment plants. Because of the chemicals in it, the sludge produced may be unfit for reuse. It then needs to be handled as hazardous waste. The toxins can interfere with the workings of the treatment plants. Sometimes they kill the bacteria that digest human waste, short-circuiting the entire secondary-treatment process. Even if the treatment process works properly, many industrial toxins will remain in the effluent that gets dumped into a receiving stream because the process is simply not set up to deal with these pollutants.

Many industrial plants make use of pretreatment systems to avoid these problems. Such systems are specially tailored to remove particular pollutants from a specific business's waste stream.

However, as Daniel Weiss of the Izaak Walton League of America says, most pretreatment systems "are designed to do the minimum—like protect a treatment plant from exploding—but not really to ensure that toxins aren't passing through the plant and into the receiving waters."

Fertilizing the Land with Wastewater

Wastewater can also be spread out on land, where bacteria naturally present in the soil will decompose wastes.

In Muskegon County, Michigan, sewage is sent to lagoons where bacteria go to work on it. After a time, the water goes on to a second lagoon, where further settling occurs. After a time this nutrient-rich water is used to fertilize and irrigate 5,000 acres (2,000 hectares) of feed corn. The soil, which is called a "living filter," finishes the treatment process. As the water percolates down through the soil, it is captured in drains that carry the now-clean water to nearby lakes and streams.

The Muskegon system, and others like it, is an example of a *positive farm-city loop*. While other places find farmers

In a farm-city loop, treated wastewater from the city can be piped to farms for use in irrigating crops. The crops are then returned to the city.

and city dwellers in competition for scarce water resources, municipalities that use land treatment of wastewater find that it meets the needs of both groups. The city gives the farm nutrient-rich water, eliminating the need to look for other water resources as well as the need for artificial fertilizers. The farm produces food, feed, and fiber, which it sends to the city. And the city is saved from polluting rivers and lakes with its sewage water and sludge, which saves money and the environment.

Septic Systems

A septic tank and soil absorption field are the most common form of wastewater treatment for individual homes not hooked up to municipal systems. Wastewater flows from the house into the septic tank, which is buried under the ground several yards from the house. In the septic tank, solids sink to the bottom (sludge) and grease and soap float to the top (scum). From time to time this sludge and scum must be pumped out and disposed of. They are often sent into a municipal water-treatment plant.

From the septic tank, wastewater flows to a distribution box, which sends the water through perforated pipes underground into the absorption field. This is an area of crushed rock or gravel that filters the wastewater as it seeps down.

Septic systems often fail to clean water completely because they are improperly located (such as too close to the water table) or poorly installed. Another reason they can fail is that they bypass an important part of the "living filter," the land surface. The many types of microorganisms living near the surface of the soil never get a chance to work on the nutrients of septic waste. Likewise, the roots of grass and plants near the land surface are not given a chance to remove and use the nutrients in wastewater. These nutrients often become contaminants in groundwater.

Thinking Dirty

Dr. Joseph Rossillon, former executive director of the Freshwater Foundation in Wayzata, Minnesota, recommends that we "start thinking dirty." What he's referring to is the many ways we can use "dirty" water, saving our clean-water resources for when we really need them.

A number of 3M Company plants recycle wastewater in many ways, thus reducing freshwater consumption, raw materials usage, and wastewater treatment and sludge disposal costs. The Toro Company is sponsoring research to develop grasses that need less water and that thrive on recycled wastewater.

In Pasco County, Florida, near Tampa, some wastewater goes to percolation ponds, where it filters through land on its way to recharging aquifers. Golf courses, municipal properties such as schools and government offices, and some privately owned lands are watered with partially treated wastewater. The watering also recharges water sources.

Many people believe that at least part of the answer to the water crisis lies in finding more creative ways to treat and reuse wastewater.

Chapter 6

Taking Care of Our Water

TAKING CARE OF WATER and treating it as a resource has allowed civilizations to grow and flourish. The mismanagement of water has caused more than one civilization to fail.

Disputes over water can lead to conflicts between water users. States squabble with states and nations are at odds over this resource. Israel and Jordan, Egypt and Ethiopia, India and Bangladesh are just some examples of countries that are arguing over water rights.

Water management includes all the ways we deal with water quantity. It is how we go about getting water where we need it when we want it. Many of the world's most serious problems, such as overpopulation, poverty, and pollution, affect water management. The goal of good water management is to satisfy the need for water without harming the environment or the economy.

It is easy to see that quality and quantity go together here. Where water treatment is inefficient or nonexistent, the result is dirty, polluted water, and having dirty water can really be like having no water at all.

United Nations figures indicate that at least 1.7 billion people do not have an adequate supply of drinking water. At least 30,000 people die *every day* in the poorer parts of the world because of lack of water or unsanitary water. That's about 10 million needless deaths every year.

FACT

Millions of people die each year from lack of water or waterborne disease. Young children and old people are

Ethiopian children crowd around water taps at a famine relief center that was opened during a long period of drought. Without enough water, there cannot be enough food.

especially vulnerable. Over half of the people in Third World countries do not have enough water. Sadly, efforts to bring more water to the people, such as dams and reservoirs and irrigation systems, sometimes bring with them an increase in waterborne disease, negative impacts on the environment, and the need to force people out of their homes.

Americans have been practicing water management for generations. According to the Freshwater Foundation, Americans have built 2 million dams, dried up 100 million acres (40 million hectares) of wetlands, and drilled millions upon millions upon millions of wells. Not all of this has been good water management.

Wells

One of the earliest ways humans managed water was by digging wells. When people learned to bring water up from deep in the ground, they freed their civilizations from having to be situated beside a body of fresh surface water.

100

Making a Well

You will need a piece of fine wire screening rolled into a cylinder about 1/2 inch (1.2 centimeters) in diameter and fastened so that it will not unroll. Place your cylinder in a tall glass or jar. Pour sand around the cylinder in the glass or jar. This is simulating a well dug in the sand. Pour water into the sand in the jar. You have now created an aquifer. Within a short period of time, water should flow from the sand (the aquifer) into the cylinder (the well).

If you withdraw water from your well, with a medicine dropper, for example, you will see how the water table drops when aquifers are used. Sprinkle more water onto the sand. You will see that it sinks and joins the other water, just as aquifers are replenished with precipitation.

Windmills and other contrivances were developed to lift water from wells and deliver it to homes and fields. The biggest windmills were about 25 feet (7.5 meters) tall and could lift about 37 gallons (141 liters) of water a minute from a depth of 70 to 80 feet (21 to 24 meters).

Along with the development of wells and windmills came the practice of irrigation. Wells made water available for farming. Irrigation made fields more productive.

Proper irrigation is an art. Just as irrigation can turn desert land into green fields, improper irrigation can turn fertile land into desert. Thanks to Roman cleverness in developing water delivery systems, much of the Middle East was a major producer of grain for ancient Rome. But when Roman society disintegrated and people stopped taking care of the water systems, this area became the desert it is today.

Irrigation, whether in North America (left) or Latin America (right), is done in whatever way is most convenient and least expensive for the area, to guarantee that there is enough food.

An important part of good irrigation practice is drainage (the removal of excess water). Plants need a balance among water, oxygen, and nutrients in the soil. Without proper drainage there is too much water and not enough oxygen. This is called waterlogging.

Irrigation water usually contains some salt. When the water is taken in by the plants, or evaporated by the sun, the salt is left behind. It forms a crust on top of the soil, making it difficult for plants to take up more water. The salination of farmland was a major factor in the fall of ancient civilizations along the Tigris and Euphrates Rivers.

The Worldwatch Institute estimates that 150 million acres (60 million hectares) of irrigated land in India, China, the United States, Pakistan, and the Soviet Union have been damaged by salination.

FACT

At its headwaters, the Colorado River contains less than 50 milligrams of salt for every liter of water. By the time it reaches the Mexican border, the river's level of salt has risen to well over 800 milligrams per liter. Water will begin to taste salty at 250 milligrams per liter. The EPA's maximum safe level for salt in drinking water is 500 milligrams.

As much as 50 percent of irrigation water is wasted through evaporation and by soaking into the groundwater. Of course, this water doesn't disappear. It will return eventually as precipitation and be withdrawn for use again, but the money and energy spent pumping it is wasted.

Some people think that government policies actually encourage such waste by providing irrigation water at unrealistically low prices. Sometimes the price the farmer pays for irrigation water covers as little as 2 percent of what the water actually costs.

Mining and Overdrafting

Heavy use of groundwater is sometimes referred to as groundwater mining because a valuable resource—water—is being removed from the Earth and put to use. Like all other mining operations, care must be taken to ensure that this resource is not exhausted or destroyed.

Overdrafting refers to the practice of taking more water from an aquifer than is naturally replenished by precipitation. Overdrafting can lead to the depletion of an aquifer.

One of the great aquifers of the United States is the Ogallala Aquifer, named for the Ogallala Sioux Indians who used to live in the area above it known as the High Plains.

As a result of irrigation water lowering Nebraska's Platte River (also shown on page 98), woody plant growth covers the sand bars. The plant growth is burned so sandhill cranes can roost at night.

The Ogallala Aquifer lies under parts of North and South Dakota, Nebraska, Kansas, Colorado, Oklahoma, and Texas. It is the water source for millions of acres of irrigated fields, where cattle graze and feed corn grows. In the 1930s there were only 170 irrigation wells on the High Plains taking water from the Ogallala Aquifer. By the late 1940s there were 8,000, and by 1957 there were 42,225 wells.

An aquifer does not necessarily have to be completely emptied to be considered depleted. The water table can drop until it is too expensive to pump it any longer. Or, in the case of aquifers along seacoasts, the water table may drop below sea level, letting salt water enter the aquifer.

Studies show that the water table under the Texas High Plains drops about 2 to 7 feet (0.6 to 2.1 meters) each year. By the year 2000 it may all be gone, or lowered to the point where it is not economically feasible to pump it.

The same is true in other places in the world. Research shows that the principal aquifers used by Mexico City drop by about 11 feet (3.3 meters) each year. The government is trying to revise its cost policies to reward conservation.

FACT

In 1991 about 70,000 ten- and eleven-year-old children acted as water inspectors, going into millions of homes in Mexico City, the most crowded and polluted city on Earth. They checked for leaks and gave out information on water conservation.

Subsidence. The pores in an aquifer are normally filled with water. When a great deal of this water is removed, the weight of the ground over the aquifer can cause the earth to

settle, and even to sink. This process is known as subsidence. There are areas around Tucson, Arizona, where the earth has sunk several feet, due to overdrafting.

A freshwater cypress swamp in Louisiana—dying because salt water has been allowed to intrude from the sea.

In the Houston-Galveston areas of Texas, water levels have declined 240 feet (72 meters) since the 1940s. In some places the land surface has sunk more than 8 feet (2.4 meters). Some of this land lies along the Gulf of Mexico, and is now subject to flooding by ocean waters.

This phenomenon is not unique to the United States. Subsidence has also damaged buildings and streets in such cities as Mexico City and Beijing, China.

This practice of withdrawing more water from aquifers than nature can replace is an example of living out of balance with water supplies. Many researchers are calling for a return to the philosophy and practice of "safe yield"—taking no more than is naturally replenished.

Obviously, we cannot eliminate irrigation if we hope to feed the growing world population. But there are ways farmers can improve the efficiency of the way they get water to plants. For example, the *drip irrigation system* developed by the Israelis delivers water directly to each plant. Farmers can breed plants that tolerate less water and water of lesser quality. They can also grow crops in the most suitable climate.

This last idea seems obvious, and yet at the same time that farmers in desert states are given cheap water to grow alfalfa and cotton (extremely thirsty crops), farmers in the rainy East are being paid *not* to grow these crops.

Water Projects

Many areas of the world have established big water projects for the purpose of transporting water from places of plenty to places of need. Such projects are generally paid for with government money and cost millions, even billions, of dollars. In the United States, the largest water projects are located mainly in the Southwest.

The Colorado River Aqueduct carries water from the Colorado River to the Los Angeles area. It is made up of more than 300 miles (483 kilometers) of canals, tunnels, and pumping stations. It is one of many projects bringing water to the ever-growing Los Angeles metropolitan area. Another is the California Aqueduct, which carries Sacramento River water 500 miles (805 kilometers) south to Los Angeles.

Even this isn't enough. The Owens River Valley is now a salty desert since its water was siphoned off to Los Angeles. The waters of Mono Lake, once a haven for wildlife, are dropping and becoming contaminated with salt and chemicals, as the lake water is diverted.

Young men and women working on a river control and reclamation project in Sichuan province in China.

The poor Colorado River! There are more claims against its water than there is water. If all the people who claim to have the right to use its waters exercised those rights at one time, the riverbed would be completely dry. The delta at the mouth of the river, shown here, is already almost dry.

A number of years ago there was a plan being discussed that would funnel water from as far away as Alaska and the Canadian Rockies to southern California. Its cost would have been in the billions, and it's hard even to imagine the environmental impact of such a project, which was to have included a huge reservoir in the American Rockies.

California is not the only water-thirsty state. The Central Arizona Project is 300 miles (483 kilometers) of pipes and canals that bring 4 trillion gallons (15 trillion liters) of water a year from Parker Dam on the Colorado River to Phoenix and Tucson. It diverts water that was already in use in other states, particularly California, with the result that those states are now considering additional water projects of their own to make up for this loss.

Many of the rivers of the West are over 100 percent allocated. Such overallocation of waterways has led to "water wars," in which one user of water battles another for water rights. Often those battles are fought between states. For example, Kansas and Colorado are currently in court over rights to water in the Arkansas River. And, Nebraska and Colorado are battling over the Platte River.

Dams on Rivers

Sometimes water for irrigation comes from surface water sources, like lakes and rivers. If surface water is to be used for irrigation, it usually means that a dam or reservoir must be built to hold water that falls during the rainy season until it is needed during dry periods.

Huge dam projects were once considered the best answer to just about any water-supply problem. Dams can store water during times of plenty and release it during times of need. Such reservoirs can serve many purposes besides irrigation water supply.

A dam may provide cheap, clean energy through hydro-electric power. It may provide a reliable water source for domestic use. It may help flood control. The lake it creates may offer new water recreation opportunities. And it will provide many jobs during building and some jobs for operation and maintenance.

But there are also disadvantages to dam building. The part of the watershed that will be flooded upstream from the dam may have been home to many people, the site of ancient burial grounds, and the habitat of animals. Migrating animals can lose nesting grounds and feeding areas. Fish lose the chance to move up and down the river. A different kind of fish may find the newly created lake to be a suitable habitat, which can change the whole food chain in the ecosystem. And it will mean the loss of any river recreation that had been available upstream.

An example of a project that highlights the pros and cons

of dam building is the James Bay hydroelectric project. Located on the southeast coast of Hudson Bay in Quebec, Canada, this $100-billion project is expected to supply more than enough energy to meet Quebec's needs, with enough left over to sell to New York, Massachusetts, and other New England states. The water of three major rivers and numerous tributaries is being diverted and stored in huge reservoirs from which it can be channeled into electricity-producing turbines. Massive tracts of land have been flooded, which means the loss of many acres of forests, and the destruction of animal and human habitats. In weighing the costs to the environment against the needs of industrial societies, technology seems to have the upper hand.

Many agencies that fund such projects are beginning to think twice about building new dams. In some cases they are finding that using existing resources more efficiently can reduce the need for these billion-dollar projects.

Floods

Flooding has occurred naturally over and over again throughout history. In a flood in northern Europe in the year 1223, some 100,000 people were killed. China's Hwang Ho (Yellow) River, also known as "China's Sorrow," is notorious for periodic flooding. A single flood is said to have killed as many as a million people in ancient times. The Hwang Ho rampaged out of control in 1642, killing 300,000 people, and again in

Raging floodwater can destroy towns, farmland, highways, and lives.

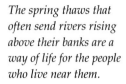

The spring thaws that often send rivers rising above their banks are a way of life for the people who live near them.

1887, when hundreds of thousands died.

Closer to home and in more recent times, American rivers are also subject to flooding. In 1965, the Mississippi River flooded its banks, submerging tens of thousands of acres of farmland in Minnesota, Wisconsin, Illinois, Iowa, and Missouri. Some 40,000 people were evacuated from their homes. While loss of life was relatively low, property damage from the flood was estimated at $200 million.

A common cause of flooding in the Northern Hemisphere is rapid thawing of snow in spring, accompanied by heavy rainfall. In the warmer parts of the world, heavy rains called monsoons often cause flooding each year. In many of these areas, people depend on these floods for the water and nutrients they bring to their soil.

In any case, flooding occurs when the amount of water in a river channel is greater than the channel can hold. Then the water spills out of its channel and onto the river's floodplain. The floodplain is the land along a river's banks that is likely to be flooded periodically. This land is often quite fertile from the sediment that floods leave behind, so farms often spring up along floodplains.

Flooding tends to be more of a problem in urban areas where people have built structures that can be damaged by floodwater. Sometimes these structures are themselves the reason for flooding. Buildings and concrete cover so much of the ground that they prevent rainwater from seeping into the soil. Rainwater then runs quickly into local surface waters, which overflow their banks, flooding streets and homes. It also runs into storm sewers, which may or may not be able to handle this sudden surge of water. Often this excess water overloads water-treatment plants, resulting in untreated or partially treated sewage/rainwater being dumped into water sources.

Urban flooding can be prevented by not allowing so much construction in floodplains, leaving unpaved areas where rainwater can be absorbed, and constructing underground drains to capture and hold rainwater. One such project is being constructed under the streets and rivers of Chicago. Called Deep Tunnel, it holds billions of gallons of rainwater until the rain stops and water-treatment plants can handle it.

Floods are a continual reminder that we will probably never really control the waters of the planet. The best we can hope for is to manage it better.

Droughts

A drought is an extended period of time when not nearly as much rain falls as is normal for a particular region. Like floods, droughts are natural occurrences that have happened throughout history. Also like floods, they can be made worse by the things people do, such as mining aquifers or draining rivers. During periods of drought, when water flow in a river or lake is reduced, conflict over water rights heats up.

After a drought has lasted a while, food prices rise, less

Drought can destroy recreation areas, as when lack of rain made these boat slips on California's Lake Cachuma (left) useless. Rains in spring of 1991 started refilling the lake. Even more important than recreation, however, is the fact that drought makes the earth too dry for crops to grow (right).

food is produced, more forests are in danger of fire, rivers get so shallow that boats can't move, there is less water for people to use, and wetland habitats are endangered.

In 1988, 35 states reported drought conditions in at least part of their state. According to many weather watchers, it was the hottest, driest year in the United States in at least the last 50 years, and one of several hot, dry years in the last decade.

Rainfall during April, May, and June of 1988 was the lowest ever recorded for the nation. June, July, and August made up the hottest summer months in 194 years of recording temperatures. The mayor of Albany, New York, stood inside his city's water reservoir, which was at its lowest point in 26 years, to dramatize the water shortage caused by the drought.

The drought and heat eased a little over the country as a whole during the summers of 1989 and 1990. But in the Southwest, conditions continued to remain abnormally dry. This situation was made worse by the fact that it followed a period of population growth and water mismanagement.

The winter of 1988/1989 was the fifth year in a row in which rain and snow in the West were below historical averages. That kept places that were dried out during the summer of 1988 from recovering, so that dry conditions in the summer of 1989 were even more serious than they would otherwise have been.

The summer of 1990 was also dry in the West. During that summer, officials all over the state of California began taking strict stands on water use. In Santa Barbara, people were not allowed to water lawns and gardens except with hand-held buckets. No new landscaping could be planted in San Clemente. In Pasadena, city workers installed a number of water-saving devices such as low-flow showerheads free of charge. Los Angeles banned serving water in restaurants except on request.

The amount of water farmers could use in the Central Valley was cut drastically. Farmers use most of the fresh water used in the West, so when water supplies are cut, many farmers are driven out of business. Those farmers who are hanging on are finding that increased water efficiency and conservation are their only hope.

Many water specialists feel that conservation will remain a critical part of life in the West if the water resources are going to meet the needs of both urban and rural water users. This highlights the fact that one of the best methods of water management is water conservation.

During the drought of 1988, barges had difficulty navigating on the Mississippi River. There was talk of releasing water from the Great Lakes to raise the level of the Mississippi River. But who had the authority to decide on such an action? Over a dozen federal agencies, several states, and even another country (Canada) have a voice in the management of the Great Lakes water involved, and they all had conflicting interests in the matter.

Such conflicting interests in conjunction with drought serve to heighten water-related conflicts in other places in the world, too. In arid southern India, fast-growing urban areas compete with farmers for meager water supplies. Frequent periods of drought mean that water supplies are shrinking even as demand is increasing. In Madras, India, each person was given a daily ration of 8 gallons (30.4 liters) of water during a dry period in the summer of 1990.

Periods of drought have had dramatic and devastating effects on Egypt, also. During the summer of 1988, drought conditions were so severe that the water level in the Nile River dropped to its lowest point in a century. This river is the only major freshwater source for Egypt's 55 million people. Lowered water levels in the river mean cities and farms must compete for reduced water supplies.

The California aqueduct system consists of many miles of concrete that carry water where it is needed. But many people in the places that that water comes from are complaining about too much water being taken.

Water Wars. There is no single water-management agency or policy to deal with water problems on a nationwide level in the United States. Instead, there are numerous (and sometimes contradictory) laws and policies at state and federal levels. This is why water wars so often bring people to court. But at least they're coming to court and not shooting it out on the banks of the river as was not unheard of in the past!

As "water wars" and drought conditions continue, "water theft" is also on the rise. Instances of landscapers hooking up to fire hydrants, and home builders bypassing water meters are reported from time to time.

As quality water becomes more difficult and expensive to get, our days of taking water for granted are coming to an end. Indeed, for some people, water has always been a precious commodity. But for too many of us, it has been so cheap and plentiful that we could waste it by the gallon.

Unfortunately, North Americans often don't seem to value something unless it is costly. Maybe if water costs more we will all value it more highly. In any case, it is likely that it will cost more in the near future, and in some places, water bills will rise a lot, perhaps as high or higher than property tax bills.

Simply shifting to a system where people are charged more for using large quantities of water would help. In the East Bay area of San Francisco, water savings were accomplished by charging a higher rate for water used over a certain amount. A number of other cities have started a similar system. But many water-supply systems, charge a *lower* rate the *more* water is used. Obviously, this doesn't encourage conservation.

Water conservation needs to become a way of life, so that water no longer is allowed to go to waste.

When the city of Tucson started its "Beat the Peak" water-conservation program, which encouraged people to conserve water, especially during "peak" or heavy use hours, average water use dropped from 205 gallons (779 liters) daily to 161 gallons (612 liters).

We have to rethink our water-management practices. There are not likely to be any new water sources to use. We have to be more careful with the supplies we have.

Chapter 7

Taking Action

Taking care of our precious water supplies is not something we can leave entirely to city officials or government agencies. There are many things YOU can do to help save our water resource.

1. Conserve water in your house in as many ways as you possibly can. Fix leaks in toilets and sinks. Place a filled plastic bottle in the toilet tank so less water is used with every flush. Take shorter showers or shallower baths. Use water-saving showerheads and low-flow faucet aerators. Don't let water run down the drain while washing dishes or brushing teeth. Compost kitchen waste rather than running an electric disposal.

2. Conserve water outdoors as well. Use landscaping techniques that require less water. Water lawns and gardens only when truly necessary and use efficient techniques (such as watering early in the morning and watering close to the ground, instead of spraying into the air). When washing cars, be sure to use a hose shut-off nozzle so that water is not wasted. Never use a hose to wash off concrete when a broom will do just as well.

3. Reduce the amount of waste you create and landfill space you require by reusing and recycling as much as possible. Fewer landfills mean less leachate.

4. Reduce the amount of hazardous chemicals used in your home. Use biodegradable, phosphate-free detergents. Baking soda is an environmentally friendly alternative to cleanser, and vinegar-water cleans windows and glass surfaces. Outside, reduce or eliminate the use of fertilizers.

5. If you must use hazardous chemicals, and it's pretty hard to avoid them altogether, make sure that they are handled and disposed of as carefully as possible. Don't use

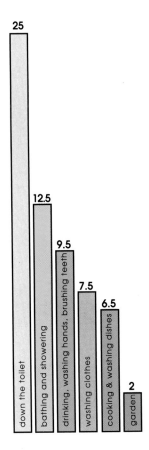

WATER USE IN GALLONS PER PERSON PER DAY IN THE MIDWEST

25 — down the toilet
12.5 — bathing and showering
9.5 — drinking, washing hands, brushing teeth
7.5 — washing clothes
6.5 — cooking & washing dishes
2 — garden

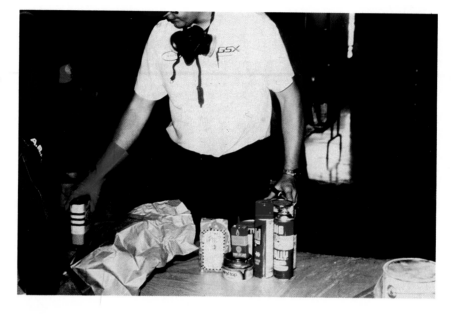

Don't pour toxic chemicals (including paint and paint thinner) down the drain and don't dispose of them with your trash. Find out about Clean Sweep Days in your community.

toilets and sinks as wastebaskets! (If your community doesn't have a program such as Clean Sweep for safe hazardous-waste disposal days, consider organizing one!) Don't pour motor oil, or any hazardous chemical, on the ground. It can too easily find its way into the groundwater. Take used motor oil to a service station for recycling.

6. Properly care for any septic system or well on your property. Such household chemicals as paint thinner, pesticides, and oil should never be put into a septic system because they might find their way into groundwater.

7. Educate yourself and others. Visit a water-supply system and wastewater treatment plant. Learn what they can handle—and what they can't. Be alert to land, air, and water abuse in your area that could threaten your water resources.

8. Adopt a body of water as described in Chapter 1. Report your findings to your class. Involve other people in

the project. The more people who are concerned about local waterways, the safer those waterways will be.

9. Find out about organizations that are working to save our water resources. For example, the National Wildlife Federation is very concerned about water pollution. They want to see all new homes and public buildings constructed with the most efficient water-conserving plumbing and appliances possible. They also want to see realistic rate structures so that consumers pay the true cost of the water they use. They are interested in promoting public awareness of water issues and encourage your involvement. For more information, you can write for a free copy of the "Citizen's Action Guide for Water Conservation," National Wildlife Federation, 1400 16th St., NW, Washington DC 20036.

In addition, write the Izaak Walton League, 1401 Wilson Blvd., Level B, Arlington, VA 22209, for their Save Our Streams Kit and *SPLASH Newsletter*.

Express Your Opinion

The water that we drink now and have available for the future is only as clean as the laws of our states, provinces, and nations force it to be. Encourage your parents and their friends to vote for officials who have a record of real action when it comes to the environment. If they are elected, check on their voting record. If they go back on their word, write and remind them of their campaign pledges.

Let your public officials, both elected and appointed, know that you are concerned about the preservation of water supplies in your area. The longer we let pollution of all kinds go on, the less likely we are to have pure water to drink in the future.

Writing Letters. In writing a letter in which you express your opinion on controversial issues, follow these seven tips:

1. Make your letter one page or less. Cover only one subject in each letter.

2. Introduce yourself and tell why you, personally, are for or against the issue.

3. Be clear and to the point.

4. Be specific on whether you want the person to vote "yes" or "no."

5. Write as an individual. The environmental groups you belong to will have already let the legislator know their stand on the issue.

6. When you get a response, write a follow-up letter to re-emphasize your position and give your reaction to your legislator's comments.

7. Write again to thank your legislators if they vote the way you asked them to.

On issues concerning state or provincial legislation or actions, you can write to:

Your local state or provincial legislator. Check at your local library to discover his or her name.

The governor of your state or premier of your province. Write in care of your state or provincial capital.

The director of your state or province's department of natural resources or related environmental agency. Check your local library for the specific person and the address.

On issues concerning federal legislation or to express your opinion about actions taken by the federal government, you can write to:

Your two state senators. Check at your library to discover their names.

The Honorable _____
U.S. Senate
Washington, DC 20510

Your local congressman. Check at your local library to discover his or her name.

> The Honorable _____
> U.S. House of Representatives
> Washington, DC 20515

Your local provincial or federal member of Parliament. Check at your local library to discover his or her name.

> The Honorable _____
> House of Commons
> Ottawa, Ontario, Canada K1A 0A6

The President of the United States. He has the power to veto, or turn down, bills approved by the Senate and the House of Representatives as well as to introduce bills of his own. He also has final control over what the U.S. Environmental Protection Agency and other agencies do.

> President _____
> The White House
> 1600 Pennsylvania Avenue, NW
> Washington, DC 20501

The Prime Minister of Canada.

> The Honorable _____
> House of Commons
> Ottawa, Ontario, Canada K1A 0A6

Join Organizations

There are many groups of people who care about protecting the water resources of our planet. They check on what is happening around the world and watch for surface and groundwater resources in danger. They also do their best to inform the general public about such things. Many of them have local chapters that welcome all the help they can get.

The following organizations are among those that play a major role in fighting to preserve our water supplies:

Canadian Wildlife Federation, 1673 Carling Ave., Ottawa, Ontario, Canada K2A 3Z1

The Center for Environmental Information, 99 Court St., Rochester, NY 14604

Environmental Action, 1525 New Hampshire Ave., NW, Washington, DC 20036

Environmental Defense Fund, 1616 P St., NW, Washington, DC 20036

The Freshwater Foundation, Spring Hill Center, 725 County Road 6, Wayzata, MN 55391

Friends of the Earth, 218 D St., SE, Washington, DC 20003

Greenpeace USA, 1436 U St., NW, Washington, DC 20009

National Wildlife Federation, 1400 16th St., NW, Washington, DC 20036

National Audubon Society, 645 Pennsylvania Ave., SE, Washington, DC 20003

Natural Resources Defense Council, 1350 New York Avenue, NW, #300, Washington, DC 20005

Pollution Probe, 12 Madison Ave., Toronto, Ontario, Canada M5R 2S1

Resources for the Future, 1616 P St., NW, Washington, DC 20036

The Sierra Club, 730 Polk St., San Francisco, CA 94109

Wilderness Society, 1400 I St., NW, 10th Floor, Washington, DC 20005

World Wildlife Fund, 1250 24th St., NW, Washington, DC 20037, or 60 St. Clair Ave., E., Suite 201, Toronto, Ontario, Canada M4T 1N5

Worldwatch Institute, 1776 Massachusetts Ave., NW, Washington, DC 20036

We all need to take a broader view of water. The farmer needs to be concerned about the topsoil that erodes from his fields and fills surface waters with sediment, and the fertilizers and pesticides that wash from his fields into water resources. The city dweller needs to think about what he puts down his drains. Septic tank users have to beware of fouling their own and their neighbors' water supplies.

We have to stop being city versus farm or state versus state or industrialized countries versus Third World nations. Water use and abuse is a global concern. There is a limited supply of water on Earth, and we must all protect it.

GLOSSARY

acid rain – rainfall, or any kind of precipitation, that is higher in acid content than normal. Precipitation with a pH (acidity measurement) below 5 to 5.6 is considered acidic. The main cause of acid rain is sulfur and nitrogen emissions resulting from the burning of fossil fuels.

acre-foot – a unit for measuring large volumes of water. An acre-foot is the amount of water it would take to cover one acre of land one foot deep with water. It is equal to about 326,000 gallons (1.2 million liters) of water.

aeration – the process of adding air to water. This is usually done by spraying water into the air so that the two can mix. It is often done as part of the water-purification process.

algal bloom – an unnatural increase in the growth of algae (small rootless aquatic plants) caused by an increase in nutrients (such as nitrogen and phosphorus) in water. It can lead to a decrease in the amount of oxygen available to fish and other life-forms in the water.

aquadynamics – a term used to describe the interrelationship between water quality and quantity in determining whether there is sufficient water for human needs.

aquifer – water-bearing rock formations. An aquifer is the space below the water table where all the pores between particles of rock are filled with water. A well sunk into an aquifer will fill with water that can then be pumped to the surface for use.

biochemical oxygen demand (BOD) – the amount of oxygen required to meet the needs of microorganisms in a particular body of water. When there is a great deal of organic matter, such as sewage, in a body of water, microorganisms need a lot of oxygen to digest it, so the BOD is very high.

carcinogen – any substance capable of causing cancer.

carrying capacity – the maximum number of people that a particular area can support without harm to the environment.

condensation – the process in which water in vapor form changes into liquid form. Water vapor in the air gathers in clouds, where it condenses into liquid and falls as precipitation.

desalination – the process of removing salt from water.

effluent – water flowing out of one source, into another, such as treated wastewater flowing from a treatment plant into a receiving stream.

eutrophication – the aging of a body of water as with overenrichment—the addition of too many nutrients. This causes a waterway to go through succession faster than it normally would.

evaporation – the process by which liquid water becomes water vapor.

groundwater – water found between underground particles of soil and rock. Groundwater is the water that supplies wells and springs.

hydrologic cycle – the water cycle—the circulation of water between the air and the ground through the processes of precipitation, evaporation, and condensation.

infiltration – water seeping from one place to another. Rainwater *infiltrates* the ground and becomes groundwater. Ocean water infiltrates freshwater aquifers if too much water is withdrawn, contaminating the fresh water with salt.

inorganic compounds – substances that are not organic, which means not containing carbon. Minerals such as iron and lead are inorganic compounds.

leachate – contaminated liquid produced by water seeping through solid waste, such as rainfall seeping through a landfill.

organic compounds – substances containing carbon. Anything composed of living or once–living material is an organic compound.

overdrafting – taking more of something than is replaced. Aquifers suffer from overdrafting when more water is pumped out than is replaced by rainfall.

permeability – the ability to let liquid flow through. Some rocks are *permeable*, meaning that there are interconnected spaces that let water flow through.

porosity – the amount of pores, or openings. A rock is highly *porous* if it has many openings between particles.

runoff – water that does not soak in, but rather "runs off" the surface of the soil into a sewer or body of water.

salinity – the saltiness of a substance.

sludge – semiliquid, semisolid matter such as material removed from wastewater during treatment. In some cases, such sludge can be used as fertilizer.

subsidence – the process in which land sinks after too much groundwater below it is withdrawn.

transpiration – the process by which plants give off water vapor.

trihalomethanes – substances formed by a reaction between chlorine and certain organic compounds sometimes found in water. The most common is chloroform. Trihalomethanes are carcinogens.

waterlogging – the process of soaking soil with excessive amounts of water. Too much water can be as damaging to plants as not enough water.

watershed – the land around a river from which water drains into that river.

water table – the top of the underground area where all spaces between soil and rock are completely filled with water.

INDEX

Bold Number = Illustration

PHOTO SOURCES

ABOUT THE AUTHOR

Eileen Lucas lives in southeastern Wisconsin with her husband and sons, Travis and Brenden. She graduated from Western Illinois University with a degree in Communications. She now works full-time writing nonfiction books for schoolchildren. In addition to *Acid Rain*, another book in the *SAVING PLANET EARTH* series, she has written biographies of Vincent Van Gogh and Jane Goodall, and a book on peaceful conflict solving.